"*In Pitch Your Business Like a Pro Victor really gets to grip with one of the most important elements of business development- selling you and your business. It gives tips on positioning yourself as a professional and the go to person in your industry. It helps you to develop that perfect pitch to pull out of your back pocket at any given time so you are always ready to sell with confidence, authenticity, gravitas and believability. Whether you are pitching for new business, funding or investors Pitch Your Business Like a Pro is a must read before starting your sales journey.*"

Dr. Yvonne Thompson
CBE Chair ACBN , UK

"*Pitch Your Business Like a Pro: Mastering the art of winning investor support for business success in six key steps*" *takes business owners deep into a discussion centred on the pros and cons of the investment options available to small businesses and how to effectively win investment funding to build a successful business. The advantages and disadvantages of angel investors, venture capitalists, crowdfunding sources are discussed and practical tips and insights are provided for preparing for that most important meeting: the pitch to investors.*

This is a highly readable book that will have immense, practical value to small business owners or entrepreneurs who are ready to expand their business."

Donna McTavish, Director
English for Business Ltd, New Zealand

"Victor has provided a great guideline for any individual or business owner ready to take their product, service or idea to the next level. "Pitch Your Business Like a Pro" offers key points and core elements to explore and incorporate into a presentation or pitch whether, formally in front of a large key audience or on the fly while networking. He manages to cover all the necessary components to assist you in your preparation as well as provide a highly organized and valuable resource that you can refer to over and over again."

Irene Kimmel
Marketing & Design Consultant
Archetype Marketing
Europe & USA

PITCH YOUR BUSINESS LIKE A PRO

Mastering The Art of Winning Investor Support for Business Success: Six Key Steps

The Entrepreneur's Guide to Secure Funding from Angel Investors, Venture Capitalists, Crowdfunding Sources and More

Victor Kwegyir – MSc
International Business Consultant,
Coach & Speaker

To: Ms ANETTE WUTOH

6/12/14

Pitch Your Business Like a Pro
© 2014 by Victor Kwegyir

Published by VicCor Wealth Publishing
www.vikebusinessservices.com

First Edition
ISBN: 0956770630
ISBN-13: 978-0-9567706-3-9
ISBN-13: 978-0-9567706-4-6 (E-book)

Printed in the United Kingdom
and the United States of America

To request Victor for speaking engagements, interviews, proposal writing, coaching or consultation services, please send an email to:
victor@vikebusinessservices.com

Victor's books are available at special discounts when purchased in bulk for promotions or as donations for educational and training purposes.

Dedication

I dedicate this book to all entrepreneurs and aspiring entrepreneurs seeking valuable support to make their business dreams a success, and to all my beautiful nieces and handsome nephews—Nana Efia Serwaa Fordwuo, Maame Abena Antwiwaah Osei-Fordwuo, Oheneba KB Osei-Fordwuo, Jessica Boachie-Danquah, Jerry Boachie-Danquah Jr., Delasi Kobla Kutsienyo, David Sarfo and Evangel Agyemang-Yeboah - who I believe will grow to become great entrepreneurs and business owners of their generation.

ACKNOWLEDGMENTS

My first passion is sharing quality information that inspires readers and informs them in their quest to find meaning in their life and success in fulfilling their business dreams. Many people have also inspired, supported and encouraged me over the years to make this passion my life's work. To all these great pillars along the path of my life and professional journey, thank you very much.

Thank you to my pastor, Pastor Matthew Ashimolowo, President and Senior Pastor of Kingsway International Christian Centre (KICC), for who you are and your great support, encouragement and inspirational teachings that constantly stir and help quicken us even when we feel like throwing in the towel. I am so blessed to sit constantly at your feet to learn, not to mention the great platform opportunities you gave me when I was unknown professionally. I am so grateful and will forever be.

Thank you to Pastor Ade D'Almeida of KICC for the awesome support, counsel, thoughts and shared ideas, each of which has been exceptionally helpful and made the journey worthwhile.

Thank you to Mr. Godfrey & Mrs. Kemba Agard, also of KICC. You have become a great friend, encourager, supporter and an immense help. Only the Lord, whom we serve continually, can help me appreciate you.

Thank you to my great friend Michael Ajose, a Technical Analyst at the London Stock Exchange. Your friendship, prayers, encouragement, thoughts and help are always very much appreciated.

Thank you also to Dr. Thomas Lawrence, Chairman, Omega-Butler International - London, Fort Worth, Hong Kong, Port Harcourt; Thank you also to Mr. Sam and Mrs. Vero Acquaye, Director of Finance & Administration, Universal Merchant Bank Ltd., Accra, Ghana; Mr. Atto Esiam, Head of Operations, TF Financial Services, Accra, Ghana; Mr. Thomas and Mrs. Wilhelmina Andoh, East Hampton, Connecticut, USA; Mr. Kennedy and Mrs. Sarah Dosomah, Cardiff, Wales; Ms. Bridget Bempong, Tema, Ghana; Mr. Olayinka & Mrs. Oluwakemi Babtunde of Dominionglow Ltd., London, UK; Minister Joseph & Mrs. Bunmi Adaran, KICC, London, UK; Mr. & Mrs. Akinleye Olu-Philips, CEO & Director, PDR Media Services, Lagos Nigeria; and Ms. Annette Wutoh, London, UK. Most of you will never know the full extent of how something you said, shared, helped me with or provided for me contributed to my ability to write this third book.

Thank you to my immediate family: Mr. Sylvester and Mrs. Theodora Osei-Fordwuo, owners of the Afrikan Grill, Aurora, Colorado, USA; Ms. Natalia Kwegyir, Ghana; Mr. Jerry and Mrs. Dorothy Boachie-Danquah, Ghana; Mr. Lawrence and Mrs. Marian Kutsienyo, Ghana; Mrs. Coretta Kwegyir, my wife; and Mrs. Agnes Kwegyir, my mum, USA. I appreciate you all for your love and prayers. May God richly bless you.

Thank you to my valuable clients for the great experience I've gained in working with you.

Above all, thank you to God and Jesus Christ, my Lord and personal saviour, who is my source of life, my constant inspiration, my strength, my guide and the provider who makes all things possible for me.

CONTENTS

INTRODUCTION

Pitching is part of business and life as a whole. We pitch our skills to employers for that job opening we so desire, we pitch our products or services to clients to win their hard earned cash and our business or ideas to investors and potential partners to win much-needed support, collaboration or an injection of vital funds for growth and expansion of the business.

Most people, however, find even the thought of pitching an idea daunting and would give almost anything not to have to do it. But new entrepreneurs, especially, need to learn the art of pitching effectively in order to win investor backing to move them forward toward the realization of their business dreams.

Anyone interested in becoming an entrepreneur or owning a business has probably watched TV shows such as *Shark Tank* (USA) and *Dragons' Den* (UK) where entrepreneurs pitch their ideas and businesses to established, self-made millionaires and billionaires. While a few participants end up bagging a deal with these investors, many others end up infuriating the panel by failing to answer vital questions, overlooking essential basic facts in their pitch or simply being unprepared for any meaningful dialogue with the experienced panel of investors. Many of these problems could have been avoided if a little more effort had been applied and expert guidance sought on how to manage the pitch to their advantage to secure the valuable investment lifeline or much-needed partnership. Of course not all failed pitches mean the person pitching didn't do a good job, just as not all well-presented pitches result in getting an investor on board. However, as Shark Tank and Dragons' Den vividly demonstrate each week, having a well-crafted and well-presented pitch can dramatically increase the chance of success.

Business pitching opportunities have become somewhat more common due to the popularity of these TV programs, with corporate entities and grant organizations sometimes embarking on pitching competitions in which individuals or organizations pitch their business ideas or social enterprise vision for cash and mentorship support. *The London Evening Standard* newspaper, for example, sponsored the Frontline London Campaign, a series of pitching sessions, to find 10 social entrepreneurs to back financially from among youths with troubled backgrounds in the UK. The US-based Black Enterprise website and magazine, which encourages black entrepreneurship, sponsored the Best Pitch Contest to give budding entrepreneurs the chance to pitch their business ideas before a panel of angel investor judges and a live audience with the hopes of winning valuable prizes and business resources.

While these programs and competitions have added some opportunities for pitching and receiving funding for social enterprise and business ideas, they have also lead to an exponential growth in the number of new ideas and businesses, as well as expanding existing businesses. At the same time, disruptions in the global economy in recent years have significantly limited the availability of cash and capital from traditional sources, such as bank loans, loans from family or friends and personal savings, to fund new ideas and businesses. The shaky economy, as is often the case, has also led to the creation of alternative funding options and platforms. This increase in funding sources, while positive overall, continues to complicate the process of creating the most effective pitch for the right audience. For all of these reasons, it is becoming increasingly necessary for entrepreneurs, small businesses and even larger, well-established businesses to learn how to make effective pitches to take advantage of various funding opportunities.

This book arms you with the techniques necessary to effectively pitch your business and entrepreneurial ideas anytime an opportunity comes your way to do so. It is designed to help you to explore which options are best for you and how to position yourself to pitch *you*, your *idea* and *your business* to potential investors. To do this most effectively, it is important to know to whom you are pitching to, what they look for in a winning pitch, and how to best deliver it.

As an established entrepreneur and business professional who has made a significant number of pitches and has helped prepare others do so over the years, I've designed this book to help you successfully address these questions by:

- Discussing the major funding options, investor groups and platforms available to the entrepreneur.

- Offering a complete guide to creating a compelling business plan as a basis for developing an outstanding pitch.

- Providing a valuable list of the essential do's and don'ts of pitching.

This book also shows you what to aim for in a pitch and what investor audiences look for in a pitch, as well as offering a master-class in how to deliver a pitch that you can use to develop your own winning pitching style. At the end of the book is a *bonus chapter* with precise details on how to make a successful sales pitch.

Your ability to pitch effectively will go a long way toward making your business dream a success, especially when you are able to attract the right kind of investor who is not just keen on making some money from your business but believes in you and your journey.

Welcome to *Pitch Your Business Like a Pro!*

PART I

THE ART OF PITCHING

CHAPTER 1

WHAT IS PITCHING?

Delivering a perfect pitch is a skill every person needs, especially entrepreneurs and business owners. To shy away from or ignore the need to learn how to pitch yourself, your ideas or your business is to limit your ability to take advantage of opportunities as they present themselves in either planned or chance situations.

Choosing to read this book tells me that you are looking forward to making a pitch, have already pitched an idea or business or are seeking to understand what pitching is all about and how to position yourself to master the skill. The fact of the matter is that all of us will have to formally pitch something at some point in our lives if we haven't done so already.

What is pitching then? Here is how I define it:

Pitching is the art of making a presentation in person, writing or via video to persuade an individual or audience to support your vision, buy your products or services, or choose you to do a job or invest in your idea or business.

To make a successful pitch requires the ability to clearly articulate your proposition to attract the interest of the person or group whose support, approval or investment you seek. It also requires the ability to sum up the unique aspects of your skills, products or services in a way that excites your audience enough to want to listen to what you are offering and to give you their full backing or to choose you above others for business, employment or other opportunities.

What we think of as a typical business pitch today usually takes the form of an entrepreneur or group of entrepreneurs presenting their idea or business to prospective investors to win their support for cash investment to develop the idea further or expand and grow the business. Although the phrase business pitch seems to have gained much popularity in the last couple of years with the advent of entrepreneurial business shows on prime-time TV, such as ABC's *Shark Tank* (US) and the BBC's *Dragons' Den* (UK), the art of pitching is not a new phenomenon. In fact, it has been a part of life for as long as humans have been interacting, we've just known it by a lot of different names and in a variety of situations that may or may not be business related.

> *Pitching is the art of making a presentation in person, writing or via video to persuade an individual or audience to support your vision, buy your products or services, or choose you to do a job or invest in your idea or business.*

A careful look back through your life will bring to mind times you've had to pitch something, whether it was selling an idea or skills to win a favor, collaboration, cash support or simply approval to go ahead with what you wanted to do. A few examples that might come to mind include:

- Pitching to your mother to let you walk to school alone for the first time, or to the school assembly or your classmates to vote for you to become a class representative or school president.

- Pitching to someone to go out on a date with you for the first time.

- Pitching your talent at an audition for a role in a play or at a tryout for a place on a team.

- Pitching your skill and expertise as a professional to gain a project assignment or contract, or to employers at interviews to secure a job.

- Pitching a concept in the workplace to management on behalf of your team or department as part of the organization's strategy.

- Pitching to clients, customers and buyers to spend their hard-earned cash on what you have to offer, or to suppliers to win their trust and cooperation for better supplier relationships and terms.

- Pitching your not-for-profit vision or cause to grant providers and organizations to gain support for the cause.

- Pitching your business idea or your existing business to obtain a loan, win investor support or gain potential partners to inject funds for growth and expansion of the business.

This book focuses primarily on the business pitch described in the last couple of items listed here. However, the techniques I will be sharing can also be put to use to help you deliver an outstanding and winning pitch in any situation.

From experience I've also found that although the concept of pitching is fairly well understood, a lot of entrepreneurs do not fully appreciate how significantly it can impact their business success. Some think of it strictly as pitching to investors and thus overlook its importance in countless aspects of business beyond seeking investor support. Some of the ways delivering a great pitch can benefit you and your business are:

- Instilling confidence in your listeners that you know what you're doing.

- Generating excitement about your business among potential investors, partners or clients, thus opening the door for greater opportunities.

- Enabling you to win over investors willing to infuse your business with the cash and backing it needs.

- Making you and your business attractive to other brands and businesses for collaboration and partnership opportunities.

- Giving your existing clients information that may make them want to pitch you to others as your enthusiasm and knowledge rubs off on them.

- Making your business stand out from the others in the eyes of those to whom you're pitching.

- Setting you up as the standard or benchmark in your field rather than the follower. As James Humes, an author and former presidential speechwriter, rightly puts it, *"The art of communication is the language of leadership."*

- Winning you increased business and revenue with an opportunity to charge premium prices.

Some entrepreneurs and business owners mistakenly restrict their idea of pitching to what is now widely known as the elevator pitch, missing out on the many broader opportunities that can derive from a more fully developed and convincingly delivered pitch. Of course the elevator pitch should not be discounted. Widely attributed to Ilene Rosenzweig and Michael Carus, this concept suggests that it should be possible to deliver a powerful and concise description of you, your company or your product in the brief timespan of an elevator ride, or approximately two minutes. **The Cambridge Business English Dictionary** defines the elevator pitch as *"a short description of a product or business idea, especially one given to a possible investor."*

While at times such a brief description might be the only opportunity you have to give a pitch, in most cases it should serve as merely the starting point of a much more thoroughly developed process. Hopefully, this type of short introduction to your idea or business will relay just enough information to cause your listeners to ask you to tell them more.

No matter how great your idea, it's not a business until you build it into one.

The first couple of minutes of a pitch are in fact vital and can be a deciding factor in the presentation as a whole. However, most pitch sessions are much longer than this and require extensive preparation and planning as well as precise and clear delivery to grab the audience's attention, convince them to buy into the business prospects and win them over for the support or cash injection you need.

Deborah Meaden, a Dragons' Den millionaire investor, once said, *"Having a great idea is fantastic, but there's a very big difference between an idea and a business."* In other words, no matter how great your idea, it's not a business until you build it into one. To create a successful business out of an idea or concept requires serious effort and in most cases some form of support, partnership or collaboration. Entrepreneurs need to learn the art of pitching so they can win the support they need, get the right people (investors and partners) on board, win client business and ultimately build a successful business.

> *Entrepreneurs need to learn the art of pitching so they can win the support they need, get the right people (investors and partners) on board, win client business and ultimately build a successful business.*

Though the general concept of pitching is the same no matter who the audience is, the type and extent of the content varies dramatically between consumers and investors or potential partners. Whereas consumers are simply interested in the benefits the service or product will give them in meeting their needs or solving their problem, investors and potential partners are nearly always interested in extensive details about the business that help to indicate its viability and profitability. Some of the many aspects of your business that you'll need to be prepared to discuss during a pitch to investors, potential partners or your bank are:

- the product or service offered by the business;
- the unique selling point of the product or service;

- the market;
- the target customer;
- the competition;
- your management team
- your business model.

Before delving further into the art of delivering a perfect pitch (Part 4 of this book), I'd like to first walk you through a few basic but important subject areas necessary to equip you to pitch any business, idea, skill or vision to potential investors, partners or grant providers to win their support and cash. Delivering the perfect pitch hinges on your ability to appreciate and understand these next few chapters and how to take advantage of them to prepare and position yourself for a "pitch perfect" delivery.

CHAPTER 2

THE ENTREPRENEUR'S CHALLENGE

From originating an idea to becoming an entrepreneur to owning a successful business is a process. Not everyone is able to make it through this process as smoothly as others. While some are gifted with the ability to originate ideas, some will struggle to go beyond that point. Others, however, will manage to initiate and navigate the early stages of the start-up process until they find their feet. I believe it's at this stage that an entrepreneur is born.

An *entrepreneur*, defined in simple terms, is a person who originates an idea then goes on to initiate and navigate the processes necessary to get a business started.

Entrepreneurs are change agents, people who don't see the world as it is but as it could be. They go out and create a better world rather than sitting on the sidelines wishing for one or expecting others to do it. Entrepreneurs are always thinking ahead and continually push themselves to become better until they make a difference.

An entrepreneur is a person who originates an idea then goes on to initiate and navigate the processes necessary to get a business started.

Trust me, anyone who is able to get a business in motion has a story to tell. Chances are, the successful entrepreneur probably began the journey with a well-thought-out plan and lots of preparation. But a good start to a business doesn't necessarily mean having everything in place from the beginning. In fact, that almost never happens! As advertising expert and motivational author Paul Arden put it, *"Too many people spend too much time trying to perfect something before they actually do it. Instead of waiting for perfection, run with what you've got, and fix it along the way."*

An attribute of entrepreneurs is their ability to start a business under some of the most imperfect and unsupportive conditions.

Waiting for exactly the right conditions and support has never created entrepreneurs. An attribute of entrepreneurs is their ability to start a business under some of the most imperfect and unsupportive conditions. They are able to do so because of their drive and vision for the future of the idea and business. The strength of their drive and vision is what leads them to creative ways to navigate the inevitable early-stage obstacles and challenges and clear the way for the business idea to take off.

Among the most common challenges every entrepreneur faces is *funding*. It's almost impossible to find an entrepreneur who did not have to deal with this challenge at some point in launching a business. Unfortunately I have encountered many people who have allowed the funding challenge to become a near-crippling factor in the pursuit of their business dreams. Funding looms so large in their business vision that it blocks them from seeing anything beyond their original idea. I have come to believe that, apart from fear, becoming overwhelmed by the funding challenge is one of the most limiting factors in people's pursuit of their entrepreneurial dreams.

On a significant number of occasions at seminars, in coaching and consultation sessions and on social media chat platforms, I've had to help attendees and clients come to terms with the fact that funding should not be the first consideration when weighing up options for becoming an entrepreneur or starting a business. Rather, the first steps to undertake on the way to realizing business dreams are usually doing research, seeking expert professional advice and then using all of this information to begin planning. These steps often cost significantly less than one might imagine. Interestingly, when done right, these first steps can actually expose the emerging entrepreneur to countless cost-cutting measures, opportunities and resources for starting and growing a business.

> *Funding should not be the first consideration when weighing up options for becoming an entrepreneur or starting a business. Rather, the first steps to undertake on the way to realizing business dreams are usually doing research, seeking expert professional advice and then using all of this information to begin planning.*

It might be surprising to many who are struggling to start a business to learn that potential investors are often encouraged to see entrepreneurs who have creatively used funding problems as stepping stones to solve some of their initial challenges. Successful businesspeople and investors know well how many would-be entrepreneurs allow funding limitations to constrain their vision and curb their original enthusiasm and drive, so those who push through these challenges are at the same time demonstrating that they have the drive to succeed.

The thing about challenges in life is that it all depends on who's looking at them. What one person looks at and cries, Obstacle! Problem! Impossible! Another shouts, Opportunity! Potential! Advantage! It all comes down to perspective.

The thing about challenges in life is that it all depends on who's looking at them. What one person looks at and cries, Obstacle! Problem! Impossible! Another shouts, Opportunity! Potential! Advantage! It all comes down to perspective.

In my first book, *The Business You Can Start*, I highlighted the advantages that even an economic downturn can offer to those paying attention to the possibility of new opportunities. This perspective is backed by extensive research of several economic downturns by economic experts over the years. My coauthor and I stressed this same perspective in my second book, *You've Been Fired! Now What?* We did so by offering numerous examples demonstrating that being laid off or unemployed can instinctively inspire people to start a business. In fact, my coauthor and I are both prime examples of this—not because of luck or unusual abilities, but because we each chose to maintain a positive perspective and stay open to possibilities we might never have considered if not faced by life's challenges.

Another point worth noting is that humans have always had the knack for rewriting "the order of things" in the face of challenges. That is why it is not surprising to read of record numbers of startups in the face of economic downturns and shaky economic periods, or to learn of the emergence of alternative ways of solving business problems, such as the creation of new funding platforms and ways of accessing these platforms by entrepreneurs—all things that one would not have imagined could be possible just a few years ago. In each case, entrepreneurs faced the challenges of hard economic times and funding limitations and found ways to turn those challenges into business opportunities.

In the simple definition of an entrepreneur that I offered at the beginning of this chapter, I noted that having a business idea is just the beginning of the entrepreneurial journey. Maintaining the vision and drive to keep that idea alive despite the inevitable obstacles along the way to actually getting a business off the ground is every entrepreneur's challenge.

The aim of this book is to teach you how to pitch your business like a pro. Top notch pitches are developed to appeal to a very specific audience—often a potential business-funding source. Successful pitches are based on thorough research and planning. Therefore, in the next section (Part 2) we'll explore the various funding options available to you for meeting the funding challenges of your startup or existing business, and in Part 3 we'll outline the essential elements for creating a strong business plan. If you have already fully researched funding options and made up your mind about which options are best for you, feel free to skip ahead to Part 3 – *Creating a Compelling Business Plan*. You may also skip to Part 4 – *Master-class Pitching Techniques* if you have identified a funding option, created a compelling business plan and are ready to learn how to *Pitch Your Business Like a Pro* to win investor funding and support for your business.

PART 2

FUNDING

CHAPTER 3
THE FUNDING OPTIONS

"If you've got a good idea, market, and team, raising money won't be your problem."

Sam Altman
Cofounder of Loopt and
President of Y Combinator

In all the years I've been in business, I have not spoken with a single entrepreneur, small business owner or even an executive at an existing corporate entity who did not have a funding need to launch a product, carry out an expansion program or just keep the business on its strategy and growth track at some point along the line. Funds are always needed to launch a new idea or business, or to meet cash flow or working capital requirements, embark on a promotional campaign or purchase fixed assets and infrastructure for a business. A common responsibility that all of these business people share is determining what funding platforms will best suit their business needs and how to pitch their business to attract the kind of funding, investment or partners that will fit into their business philosophy or ethos.

According to the European Commission, Small and Medium Enterprises (SMEs) account for 99 percent of businesses and 67 percent of all employment in Europe. And according to the European Central Bank, the availability of bank loans and the banks' willingness to lend to SMEs declined sharply after

2008, by 23 percent and 29 percent respectively. Over the same period, the value of required collateral increased by 34 percent and interest rates increased by 54 percent for SMEs. The funding gap for wealthier economies such as France, Germany, Italy, Spain and the UK is expected to increase to EUR 2.5 trillion by 2020, while most economies with less developed financial markets suffer from even greater gaps.

Funding sources are often classified into different categories such as traditional and nontraditional, internal and external, and equity and debt funding sources.

For entrepreneurs trying to get a new business off the ground, sourcing of funds can be even more challenging due to the lack of a proven track record or collateral. Although there are still funds available for those who are starting a business, entrepreneurs need to know where to look and how to think strategically and creatively in order to access those funds. It is often a good idea to take advantage of a combination of two or more funding sources, when possible, to raise the finances needed to fund a business.

As you begin to look at funding options, it is important to ask yourself the following questions:

- ▣ Can you find a lender with likeminded values?
- ▣ Are there informal as well as formal sources of funding available to you?
- ▣ Should you consider both unregulated and regulated funding institutions or sources?
- ▣ What is the interest rate on the amount to be borrowed?

- What are the repayment terms and time period?
- Does the institution or source of funding have an interest in businesses of your size and type?
- Does the institution or source of funding have an interest in servicing the various credit and noncredit needs of your company over time?
- Does the institution or source of funding have financial stability capable of meeting your funding requirements?

Funding sources are often classified into different categories such as traditional and nontraditional, internal and external, and equity and debt funding sources.

In the next few chapters we will look at the major sources of funding available to entrepreneurs and small business owners as they seek to successfully launch and grow their businesses. Throughout our discussion of funding platforms, it is essential to keep in mind that all funding options have their pros and cons. *You should always thoroughly familiarize yourself with all terms and conditions before signing a contract or agreeing to the specific terms of any funding facility. Engaging reputable professional advisors such as business consultants, lawyers or accountants can go a long way toward helping you understand the fine print and make the right decisions for your specific needs.*

> *Throughout our discussion of funding platforms, it is essential to keep in mind that all funding options have their pros and cons.*

CHAPTER 4

BOOTSTRAPPING

"Nothing happens until someone sells something."

Jim Barksdale, former CEO of Netscape

An approach to funding a business that has probably been around since the beginning of business itself is *bootstrapping*. Bootstrapping is basically derived from the expression "lifting oneself up by one's own bootstraps." In other words, bootstrapping is raising yourself up by your own means—in this case, funding your business from your own sources, which may be quite limited. Often an entrepreneur may have no savings or minimal funds to rely on. What sets bootstrapping apart from other forms of business funding is that it relies heavily on entrepreneurs' frugal thinking, creativity, thriftiness, planning and cost-cutting efficiency skills. Because of the limited resources at their disposal, bootstrapping

What sets bootstrapping apart from other forms of business funding is that it relies heavily on entrepreneurs' frugal thinking, creativity, thriftiness, planning and cost-cutting efficiency skills.

entrepreneurs have to creatively seek out ways to make the most of the few resources at their disposal and start making money by selling their product or service.

Here are a few ways that you might use bootstrapping to help get your business off the ground.

- Barter for goods and services when possible, offering your services, products or time in exchange for what you need.

- Hunt for bargains and buy on promotion or take advantage of limited-time price offers.

- Use your own space, such as a garage, and your own furniture, personal computers, freezers, vehicle and other such items instead of buying new ones for the business.

- Take advantage of trade credits from suppliers. This might require you to pitch your business proposition and share your business plans with suppliers to help them understand how they'll benefit as your business grows.

- Use letters of credit from customers to obtain financing. This may also take the form of acquiring some customers who are willing to pay you in advance for your products or services, which then gives you the opportunity to use their money to purchase supplies or inventory before selling them on.

- List potential startup costs and come up with less costly alternatives to each of them.

- Break down the startup process into smaller, more manageable stages to execute. It might require a bit more discipline and a longer time to "take off," but it also lowers your risk of crashing before you get the business off the ground.

- Take advantage of technology – free software, apps and platforms—to do more with less. For example, take advantage of social media platforms instead of embarking on a costly marketing or promotional campaign.

- Team up or partner with others who have complementary businesses for your target market. Of course, careful research into a potential partner's business, values, work ethic, motivation, drive and vision is necessary *before* entering into such a partnership to ensure you have a perfect fit for your business.

- Look for shared office space to work from or storage space for storage of your raw materials or products. In the UK some entrepreneurs and small businesses who are unable to afford their own business premises have rented storage spaces in some of the major Storage Centers around the country and they operate their businesses from these lots, significantly cutting down on the cost of leasing or buying a building.

- Ask for help from friends who you know and who want you to succeed. For example, they might be willing to lend you unused equipment they have or volunteer to help you out in their spare time. Or they might let you utilize their contacts, of course with their express permission.

■ Seek out local government initiatives where some business centers or districts are designated to help small businesses by offering such things as free office space, access to free Internet and workshop facilities.

Bootstrapping really begins and ends with an entrepreneur's attention to careful management of limited time and very minimal resources to start and grow a business. Most entrepreneurs end up with plenty of stories about bootstrapping strategies they employed in starting their business. Although it can slow down the growth of the venture, bootstrapping also offers a number of advantages, such as forcing you to bag some sales and sign up clients as soon as possible, ensuring that you maintain full control of the business, allowing you to avoid the stress of being accountable to anyone else and letting you grow the business at your own pace and convenience. I've always believed that bootstrapping is part of every real entrepreneur's DNA and journey.

I'm fascinated by the stories of creative bootstrapping strategies employed by some of today's best-known entrepreneurs and businesses. Apple cofounders Steve Wozniak and the late Steve Jobs' use of bootstrapping at an early stage in their partnership always inspires me.

In Jessica Livingston's interview with Steve Wozniak for her book *Founders at Work*, Wozniak recalled, *"I was good at making things with very few parts by using all sorts of tricks—almost the equivalent of mathematics—so I valued products that were made with very few parts. That helped in two ways. When you are a start-up or an individual on your own, you don't have very much money, so the fewer parts you have to buy, the better."*

There are numerous accounts of how Steve Jobs became a master of bootstrapping strategies to fund his and Wozniak's startup because he was intent on not giving away shares in exchange for funding from investors to start and grow their business. As we all know now, Apple grew to be one of the most valuable companies on earth.

The Apple story is just one of countless examples of bootstrapping by seed or early-stage startups. Most entrepreneurs, including myself, need to bootstrap at some point in their business career. When faced with limited resources, let your creativity and thriftiness kick in to enable you to make good your dream. Bootstrapping will let you start now, regardless of what you have or do not have by way of funds.

I believe bootstrapping is a test of the entrepreneurial spirit in a person and necessary for business success in the long run. Whereas some deliberately avoid taking investor cash in an attempt to control the direction of their companies and focus on product development and testing of the market, most entrepreneurs bootstrapped at some point, if not during the early stages of their business. Having said that, there is equally great reward in seeking investor support as you can benefit from their advice and opinions and their networks in growing your company.

Tech PR entrepreneur and angel investor Zach Cutler says it best, *"Bootstrapping makes you grow as a person. It's tough, stressful and full of ups and downs. And those things teach you invaluable lessons."*

CHAPTER 5

Personal Savings and Credit

Using your own funds can be a cost-effective way to raise capital for your business. According to Thisismoney.co.uk, two out of three small businesses in the UK were started with their founders' own money. And according to data compiled by Fundable.com, a crowdfunding website, in 2013 up to 57 percent of startups were funded by personal loans and credit in the US.

Personal resources can include bank savings, shares or stocks, redundancy money, profit sharing or early retirement funds, real estate equity loans or cash value insurance policies. If you have been able to accrue enough resources to enable you to fund your business, why not? Not only does it give you peace of mind, it also means you do not have to answer to anyone or part with any percentage of ownership, giving you total control of the business.

Pledging your own assets as collateral, which often tends to be your home, is one option often considered. That, of course, means remortgaging to take out a home equity loan. Although quite tempting, this option must be carefully weighed. Professionally I will advise that your home should be your last resort for funding a business. You don't want to lose the roof over your head should the business not take off or yield enough on time to meet repayment requirements. As EasyJet founder Stelios Haji-Ioannou puts it, *"I believe one should only place bets one can afford to lose"* when funding from your own resources.

Funding from your own pocket can be a good motivator because your neck is on the line, as it were. It can also become a bonus point with investors when they consider the fact that you have put yourself fully into the business, which is a sign of your commitment to the vision and success of the business they may fund.

CHAPTER 6

FAMILY AND FRIENDS

A third potential source of funding for a new or small business is from family or friends. Often when you're just starting a business, the people who are closest to you may be the only ones who are willing to take a risk and bet on you. Because they know you and have developed a sense of personal trust or confidence in your ability over time, they have some level of assurance that they can count on you, even if they don't necessarily fully understand your idea or business concept. Especially if your business idea is untested or unproven, it can be quite challenging to get funding from traditional sources such as banks or outside investors. Having friends and relatives willing to believe in you and support you can be a great relief, even if the support is in exchange for part ownership of the business, known as *equity financing*.

In the US, according to data compiled by Fundable.com, a crowdfunding website, in 2013 up to 38 percent of startups received funding from family and friends. In the UK, according to the Family Business Network, this number is more than double with up to 75 percent of new and small businesses being funded by friends and relatives.

In addition to often being easier to get, funding from this source has other advantages as well. One of the biggest potential advantages is that you can often negotiate with family and friends to get fairly lenient repayment terms, such as low interest rates and a longer repayment period, if they choose to give you a loan rather than taking a stake in the ownership of the business.

There are generally two types of loans:

- Interest-free loans: these are less likely to have any tax implications for either you or the lender.

- Interest-bearing loans: these have tax implications for both parties. With an interest-bearing loan, you can deduct the loan interest for business purposes when calculating profit. The lender is required to declare interest received as taxable income.

It is very important to be honest and upfront with the friends and family you ask to help fund your business, explaining, for instance, why the bank turned you down for a loan if that was the case. If possible, both of you should consider the business plan carefully and objectively to assess its viability. *It is never a good idea to persuade people to lend or invest more than they can afford to lose.*

> *It is very important to be honest and upfront with the friends and family you ask to help fund your business.*

When dealing with family or friends, you should always get professional advice before you do the deal. An agreement in writing is a must and should spell out:

- The nature and timing of return on the investment and the repayment schedule, including dates, amounts and interest.

■ Respective responsibilities, such as whether the investor will have a role in the business.

■ What happens if the business goes under or fails.

■ What happens if you are unable to keep up with the repayment schedule.

An important cautionary note: money has a way of destroying even the most beautiful friendships and relationships. You certainly don't want that to happen to you and your close associates.

It can be a great relief if friends or relatives want to support you and help you get your business started without expecting you to repay the funds. Even then, however, it is always advisable that all terms of an agreement should be formally put in place in writing and signed by all parties. This is essential whether the money is being given to you as a gift, a loan or an investment.

An important cautionary note: money has a way of destroying even the most beautiful friendships and relationships. You certainly don't want that to happen to you and your close associates.

CHAPTER 7

BANK FUNDING

Banks are probably what most people think of first when considering sources of funding for a business. It is generally estimated that about 60 percent of small businesses approach their bank as their first point of call when it comes to borrowing funds for business. Banks offer long-term financing in the form of loans and mortgages, and short-term financing through credit and pre-arranged overdraft options.

Funding from banking sources often gives you more control of the business than you might have with investors or partners, allowing you to develop or expand your business as quickly as you'd like. However, you'll need to carefully consider the interest rate and terms the bank is offering, including whether the interest rate is fixed or capped. Your ability to negotiate the interest rate down as much as possible with terms to your advantage can have a significant effect on the overall cost of a bank loan.

Your ability to negotiate the interest rate down as much as possible with terms to your advantage can have a significant effect on the overall cost of a bank loan.

Banks generally look at a number of key areas when deciding to say yes or no to a business loan or overdraft request.

Ultimately the bank's goal is to determine the business's ability to generate a flow of income sufficient to enable it to service the debt according to the agreed terms after the business loan is approved.

If you plan to seek financing for your business through a banking institution, be prepared to have the bank consider the following points.

- The impression you make, including how you look and speak, and how well you develop and deliver your pitch.

- Your business plan. This should include specific details of how you plan to repay the debt.

- Collateral you can use to secure the loan, particularly if the loan is over £25,000 for most banks in the UK or if you're a new business.

- The amount of your own money you've invested in the business, which demonstrates your commitment to the business.

- Your track record with the bank, including whether you are an existing customer and have borrowed and repaid earlier loans or overdrafts.

- Existing businesses may have to show the last three years of accounts for the bank to consider historic performance details, including profits and trading history.

- Your credit rating: banks will often run a credit check on an existing business and on you personally and anyone else financially involved in the business.

With that said, it is crucial to appreciate that getting funding from banking sources has always proved somewhat challenging to entrepreneurs and small business owners due to banks' hesitancy to take on the high risks associated with the untested concepts of new businesses and their lack of a proven track record. And bank funding has become even more difficult with the advent of new regulatory requirements following the recession. Most new or early-stage startups are simply unable to meet these requirements.

Historically, banks were the only source of funding available to businesses outside personal or family resources, and many aspiring entrepreneurs and small business owners still think of them this way but fortunately, this is no longer the case. New funding options have developed in recent years that are more flexible and much friendlier than the banks, for the most part. Entrepreneurs, early-stage startup, and small business owners are increasingly shying away from the banks to focus on these alternative funding sources, some of which we'll discuss in the following chapters.

CHAPTER 8

ANGEL INVESTOR FUNDING

Angel investing is increasingly becoming one of the most significant sources of funding for startups and early-stage businesses seeking equity to grow their business. Angel investors are often high net-worth individuals who invest directly into promising entrepreneurial ventures to help them launch new businesses or grow existing small businesses. Many of these investors are entrepreneurs themselves who are now also corporate leaders and business professionals.

The quickest way for you to get a sense of this relatively new funding option for your business is to consider these basic facts about angel investing in general, how the funding is usually set up and how angel investors tend to operate in relation to the businesses they fund.

- Angel investors provide equity financing (that is, buy shares of a business, giving them partial ownership), using their own money to invest in a business.

- Business angels, as they are also known, make their own investment decisions about who or what businesses to invest in and generally engage directly in meeting the entrepreneurs. They often have entrepreneurs pitch their business to them directly.

- They usually seek active involvement, such as consulting with and mentoring the entrepreneur, thus bringing on board their experience and knowledge to help grow the business and achieve greater return on their investment.

- Angel investors also engage directly in the due diligence and investment process and are signatories on all necessary legal investment documentation.

- They often seek to have a return on their investment over a period of 3 to 8 years.

- Amounts invested are often relatively small (£5k or $7k up to £1m or $1m) compared to in-vestments frequently made by venture capitalists.

- Angel investors often offer more favorable terms than other lenders as their focus is on the entrepreneur and the overall sustainability of the business rather than simply on reaping huge profits or returns within the shortest possible time at the lowest possible risk.

- Having said that, it's important to remember that angel investors are still interested in the profitability and security of their investment and may still make the same kinds of demands that venture capitalists and other lenders may require.

- Funds provided by angel investors may be a one-off injection of seed capital or early-stage financing or ongoing support to carry the company to the next growth level or through a challenging period. Funds are often released in portions or rounds against set milestones. For entrepreneurs to get the next round of funding often requires that they first meet the previous milestone conditions.

- Business angels' interest in a business entity may sometimes go beyond just the economic re-turn from their investment to include interest in the economic development of a specific sec-tor of an economy, a particular demographic group or a geographic area where they are located.

- Increasingly, a number of angel investors are organizing themselves into syndicates, angel groups and networks to share research, pull their investment capital together and offer advice and support to their portfolio of businesses.

- Not only do they have an association that coordinates their activities, angel investors are regulated in most nations and economies. Established angel investor associations in the UK, USA, Canada, the EU and other economies also advise entrepreneurs and businesses, and oversee the general conduct of the industry and its members.

According to the UK Business Angels Associations, there are about 18,000 angel investors in the UK alone, investing an estimated £850m per annum, which is more than 2.5 times the amount of venture capital funds invested in early-stage small businesses annually. In the EU, the European Business Angels Network (EBAN) Markets and Policies report commissioned in 2012 estimated that there were as many as 250,000 business angels in the EU, and that number continues to grow. The Centre for Venture Research estimates that US angel investors invested $19 billion in 55,000 deals (about 35,000 small businesses) in 2008. It is currently estimated that about 225,000 angel investors have invested in US businesses in the last two years (2012 – 2013) alone. Some of the well-known corporate giants today, such as Google, Yahoo, Amazon, Starbucks, Facebook, Costco and PayPal, had angel investor backing in the early stages of their development before going public.

How To Access Angel Funding

To get an angel investor on board you will have to do a bit of homework to ensure you find the right investor who believes in you, your business, your values and your vision. Because most angel investors come on board with more than financial returns in mind, it's important to consider a holistic set of parameters or criteria in your search for the right investing partner for your business.

There are a number of ways to research and access angel funding.

- Speak to industry experts, associations and your own network of business professionals, and attend networking events.

- Join or link up with an angel investor network or group to find an investor. Angel networks often act as introduction agencies, matching businesses looking for finance with potential investors. They are also often able to share valuable information with you, such as the general requirements of a specific business angel.

- Identify those in the network who are interested in your line of business, stage of growth, industry, values or geographic area.

■ Find a lead investor or a group of seed investors who are willing and interested in investing in your business. The challenge entrepreneurs sometimes face at this point is coming across a number of angel investors who may ask you to find a lead investor before they come on board. This may indicate a number of things.

- The angel investors are too far away from your geographic area and would be much more comfortable if you had a local lead investor for hands-on participation and oversight.

- The typical investment of the angels you've found is less than half of your round of funds or what you require.

- They know little or nothing about your industry or market and want a lead investor more familiar with the market.

- They are not fully convinced of your company's business prospects.

If it's a case of potential angel investors having little knowledge of the market, you can go through an angel network or other sources to find investors who have backed companies in your market or similar markets before. Or you can ask the potential investors to suggest one or more angel investors who might be interested in becoming a lead, why they think those leads would be interested and whether they would be willing to introduce you to those potential lead investors.

It's a good idea to always try to find lead investors who are completely sold on your idea or business. If they are, they will often want the whole deal for themselves, decide to become a major partner or even invite others in their network to join up to fund the business.

- It's essential that you perform your own due diligence on all interested investors before becoming involved with them. For instance, the UK Angel Investor Association advises that before passing your business plan to a potential angel investor, you should ensure that the investor is self-certified as either a High Net Worth or Sophisticated Investor, as defined by the Financial Services Authority (FSA) under the UK Financial Services and Markets Act of 2000 (FSMA). In addition to ensuring that potential investors meet nationally recognized standards, it's also important to seek out other businesses they might have invested in recently to discuss those business owners' experience with the investors.

- Once you have gained the interest of an angel or angel group or syndicate, get to know their requirements.

- Prepare and pitch your business. As we've already discussed, a well-delivered pitch backed by a well-written, compelling business plan is a must to win over investors.

- Interested angels will conduct their own due diligence on you and will probably also try to get to know you better and learn more about your business proposition and model. Once they're convinced that they would like to work with you and your business, they'll negotiate a term sheet (accountants and lawyers can help you prepare it) and proceed to sign an agreement with you.

This marks the beginning of the investor relationship which usually paves the way for the release of the first round of funds to you for the business. With angel investors, entrepreneurs also gain the invaluable benefit of getting advice, mentoring and access to the investors' network to help them grow the business.

See Appendix A for a list of some of the active angel investor organizations and networks around the world.

CHAPTER 9

VENTURE CAPITAL FUNDING

Venture capital (VC) funding is financing that comes from companies or individuals in the business of investing in young, fast-growing, privately held businesses. Unlike angel investors, venture capitalists manage the pooled money of others in a professionally managed fund. Raising money for investment and making money for investors are at the core of the venture capital industry. Venture capital can be a great source of funding for startups and early-stage businesses. Most funds focus on a particular industry, geographic region, stage of development (i.e. startup or seed funding, early-stage, expansion stage and later stage) as well as the business proposition. This specialization can help you narrow down the prospects for VC funding of your business.

To gain a general understanding of VC funding options for your business consider these basic facts about how this funding is usually set up and how venture capitalists tend to operate in relation to the businesses they fund.

■ Venture capitalists provide cash investment in exchange for shares – equity financing. They like to play an active role in the invested companies through their early-stages.

■ Their major focus is to achieve the highest possible return on their investments within the shortest possible time which could be a deviation from the initial plans or ethos of the company's founders.

- VCs typically invest in high-risk companies but with potential for extensive growth. The desire for higher annual returns on their investment portfolios pushes them to favor high-risk business investments with expected returns of 50 percent or more in some cases.

- The earlier the stage of the business when the investment is made, the more equity the venture capitalists are likely to require.

- They usually don't like to participate in the initial financing of a business unless the company has a management team with a proven track record.

- VCs often prefer to invest in companies that are already profitable or have received significant equity investments already from the companies' founders.

- Venture capitalists seek to generate return by investing in startup businesses and realizing significant returns when the company goes for an initial public offering (IPO) or is sold privately in a merger and acquisition option.

- They also prefer businesses with a competitive advantage or a strong value proposition in the form of a patent, a proven demand for a product or service or a unique and protectable idea or concept.

- VCs often take a hands-on approach to their investments, requiring representation on the board of directors and sometimes being directly involved in the hiring of managers, thus providing active support by way of valuable guidance and advice to help grow and achieve greater return on their investment.

- There is a common supposition among venture capitalists that some of their business investments will yield 50 percent return or more while others will fail, which should lead to an overall portfolio yield of 25 to 30 percent per investment cycle. Many venture capitalists subscribe to the 2-6-2 rule of thumb, meaning that, on average, two investments will yield high returns, six will yield moderate returns or just return their original investment, and two will fail.

- The amount of funds VCs typically invest ranges from £300k ($500k) to as much as £200m ($350m) or even more in some unique cases.

- Not only do they have bodies or associations that coordinate their activities, VC investing is now regulated in most economies. The UK, USA, Canada and the EU all now have some form of regulation in place covering the industry and members' conduct. These groups work with governments and serve as a mouthpiece for members as well as offering advice and guidance to entrepreneurs and business owners seeking funding from its members.

- In recent decades, venture capitalists from around the world have had a huge impact on business investment. According to the 2014 Dow Jones Venture Source, in 2013, venture capitalists invested a total of US $48.5b in the global economy with a total invested rounds of 5,753. Of that amount, US venture capitalists invested $33.1b, or 68.2 percent; European VCs invested $7.4b, or 15.3 percent; Canadian VCs invested $1.0b, or 2.1 percent; Chinese VCs invested $3.5b, or 7.2 percent; Indian VCs invested $1.8b, or 3.7 percent and Israeli VCs invested $1.7b, or 3.5 percent.

In addition to the industry sector, geographic location and stage of development of a business being considered for funding, other factors can affect a VC fund's investment strategy, including:

- the amount of investment required;
- the time anticipated to a liquidity event;

- the stage of the VC fund's own life cycle. The average life cycle of a VC fund is ten years. Those funds nearing the end of this cycle are more likely to invest in later-stage deals that are closer to exit in order to quickly gain a higher potential return.

If you're interested in seeking funding from a venture capital source, bear in mind all of these factors when considering which VC funds to approach.

How to Access Venture Capitalist Funding

To access venture capitalist funding:

- Research and identify a venture capital organization inclined towards investing in your type of business or industry. Often research will be appreciated by the VCs you approach because it shows that you have thought carefully about the type of investment partner you want, are serious about the partnership and are not just seeking a cash infusion in your business.

- Establish contact within potential VC funds to familiarize yourself with their specific processes and application requirements. As part of the application process, the VC fund will usually require you to submit an executive summary of your business plan to make sure the business meets the fund's investment criteria.

▪ An interested VC fund will often request that you pitch your business to them. It is very important to adequately prepare yourself to deliver a persuasive, well-thought-out, professional pitch, highlighting your strongest value proposition and supported by a clearly articulated and compelling business plan. A well-presented pitch gives investors insight into the business and the person or team behind it, as well as some level of assurance that they know enough about you and the business to decide whether they would feel comfortable investing in your business.

▪ If your pitch heightens the venture capitalists' interest, they'll then perform their due diligence on the business, including looking in great detail at your company's management team, market, products and services, operating history, corporate governance documents and financial statements.

▪ If the VC fund remains interested after doing its due diligence, it will develop a 'term sheet' describing the terms and conditions under which the fund will make an investment. The terms are usually based on the company's performance to date, providing benefits to the business while minimizing risks to the venture fund. The investment is made in exchange for some of the company's equity.

- Once an investment has been made, which is normally distributed in rounds rather than all at once, the VC fund usually becomes actively involved in the company and remains so to the end of the agreed-upon investment period.

- As the company meets previously agreed-upon milestones, further rounds of financing are made available, with the necessary inflationary adjustments as the company continues to execute its plan.

VCs always expect to exit at some point in the business cycle, the average is after about five years. They often exit via mergers, acquisitions and IPOs, relying on their networks and experience to help the company engage the right contacts and processes to manage this transition.

As you've seen in the funding options we've considered so far, each requires a somewhat different pitching approach tailored specifically to the funding agent's needs. In the next chapter, we'll look at crowdfunding, a relatively new approach to raising funds for businesses requiring a pitch that can appeal to hundreds or even thousands of small investors online, most of whom you'll probably never meet in person.

See Appendix B for a list of some of the established and regulated venture capital organizations around the world.

CHAPTER 10

CROWDFUNDING

Crowdfunding is a financing method that involves funding a project with relatively smaller contributions from a large group of individuals rather than seeking substantial amounts from a single or a few investors.

According to the UK's FCA (Financial Conduct Authority), *"Crowdfunding is a way in which people, organizations and businesses (including business startups) can raise money through online portals (crowdfunding platforms) to finance or re-finance their activities and enterprises."*

It is increasingly becoming an important platform used by entrepreneurs and small business owners to raise funds for their business. The model allows entrepreneurs to raise money via Internet-based platforms by offering real equity in exchange for investment from a "crowd" of investors who want to invest small amounts of money to fund an idea, project, person or business. Crowdfunding platforms coordinate and administer the fundraising process, offering users valuable help in the form of tutorials via webinars and other tools in setting up a campaign.

This new fundraising model offers small business owners, who might have been turned down by banks or who couldn't meet their requirements, an invaluable opportunity to appeal directly to small investors. This also means that business investment is gradually moving from the domain of only high net worth people to anyone with as little as £5 or $5, so that nearly anyone, especially in a developed economy, can now reap the benefits of investing in a potential new business or an existing one.

A significant number of crowdfunding platforms and strategies have developed over the last 6 years, each with its own distinct focus and advantages. There are the general-purpose sites, such as Kickstarter and Indiegogo, which until recently were more reward-based sites (see the three types of sites below) where people could pledge money to new creative arts projects, an artist producing a new album or a novel technology product development project. Fundable and RocketHub are also general-purpose sites that cover a wide range of categories and are intentionally broad in scope.

Niche sites that provide narrowly focused crowdfunding services have also developed. For instance, ArtistShare caters specifically to musicians, while Gambitious is dedicated to the games industry, Unbound applies crowdfunding to book publishing, and Abundance Generation offers investors the opportunity to invest in green energy. Still other sites such as Kapipal (part of Grow VC Group) avoid categories altogether and allow users to crowdfund any project imaginable — provided it doesn't violate payment platforms terms of service.

Although our focus in this book is on crowdfunding for business, it is important to highlight work being done by other sites, such as Kiva, the pioneering crowdlending platform. Kiva works with financial institutions on five continents to provide microcredit loans to people without access to traditional banking systems. According to statistical information on its website kiva.org (August 2014), since 2005 Kiva has gathered more than 1.8 million users with about 1.2 million of them having funded loans totaling US $600,750,275.

Just Giving, another leading global donation-based crowd-funding platform, has facilitated the raising of $1.5 billion from over 21 million people for over 13,000 charities since its launch in 2001 (JustGiving.com).

The ability of entrepreneurs or small businesses to raise enough funds in the form of equity or debt financing through crowdfunding is largely dependent on them convincing enough people to contribute toward a targeted amount sufficient to meet their funding needs. In other words, a great pitch is essential for successful crowdfunding.

In addition to raising funds, entrepreneurs should also take advantage of other opportunities crowdfunding platforms offer, including:

- testing the market;

- getting valuable feedback and suggestions from "the crowd";

- gaining "the crowd" as your first line of customers who could very well end up helping you spread the word about what you are doing or intend to do in terms of your business, project or idea.

Types of Crowdfunding Platforms

According to the UK Crowdfunding Association (CFA), there are officially three different forms of crowdfunding.

Donation/Reward

On donation/reward crowdfunding sites, users give toward, or invest in, a cause such as a community park, event or program simply because they believe in it without the expectation of a financial gain. Apart from the personal satisfaction or social motivation of giving toward such a good cause, rewards can be offered to contributors, such as a ticket for an event, free gifts or acknowledgment on a plaque, book or even the cover of an album. Sites like Spacehive.com, Banktothefuture.com, Peoplefund.com, Crowdfunder.com and Crowdbnk.com are examples of donation/reward sites.

Debt

Debt crowdfunding is similar in structure to traditional private market lending schemes but in this case a company borrows money from a group of people instead of a bank or financial institution. This is also called peer-to-peer lending or lend-to-save. Apart from having contributed to the success of a venture they believe in, investors also receive adequate financial returns on the amount loaned to the business.

Investors receive their money back with interest with the applicable interest rates usually based on the risk factors associated with the business as determined by its financial data and personal securities. Debt crowdfunding platforms tend to charge lenders a fee of 1.0 – 7.5 percent per loan. The amount of interest received by lenders varies dramatically, ranging between 5 and 12 percent per year. The exception to this is in the case of microfinance, as discussed earlier in the chapter, where very small sums of money are lent to the very poor, most often in developing countries. No interest is charged on microloans, instead the lender is rewarded by doing social good.

Examples of debt crowdfunding sites include Kiva.org, Abundancegeneration.com, Lendingclub.com, Banktothefuture.com, Buzzbnk.org, Trillionfund.com and Rebuildingsociety.com.

Equity

Equity crowdfunding, also sometimes referred to as crowdinvesting, is used when an entrepreneur or business sets out to attract investment from a group of people, or "the crowd", rather than from a business angel or other private investors. This type of crowdfunding is usually subject to capital markets and banking regulations and is therefore restricted in terms of funding amounts, geography and marketing possibilities.

With this model, people invest in an opportunity in exchange for equity. Money is exchanged for a share in the business, project or venture similar to other equity funding options. The value of an investment appreciates as the business becomes successful. On the other hand, the value can depreciate due to poor performance of the business, with an investor potentially losing all their money or investment. These crowdfunding platforms make their money by charging the company raising capital transaction fees averaging 5 percent if their funding target is successfully reached. Most platforms also charge a listing fee of up to 5 percent as well as a fixed annual, monthly or one-time sum often referred to as compensation for due diligence, legal and/or compliance costs.

Equity crowdfunding sites includes Growvc.com (USA), WiSEED.com (France), Angellist.com, Fundersclub.com, Ourcrowd.com, Banktothefuture.com, Crowdbnk.com, Crowdcube.com (UK), Gambitious.com, Microgenius.org.uk, Crowdmission.com, Sharein.com, Companisto.com (Germany), Fundedbyme.com (Sweden) and Seedrs.com.

Growth and Impact of Funds Raised

By the end of 2012, there were 45 countries worldwide with active crowdfunding platforms. Currently, it is estimated that there are more than 1,000 crowdfunding platforms around the world, with 230 in Europe alone. The majority of European platforms offer hybrid investments including debt, equity and donation/reward, with 68 percent of these platforms operating across national boundaries. According to the European crowdfunding network (ECN), more than one million campaigns are estimated to have raised $2.7 billion worldwide across all types of crowdfunding platforms in 2012. Of this amount, $945 million was raised in Europe, while $1.6 billion was raised in the US. The estimated total market for 2013 is over $5.1 billion, almost double the 2012 figure. More specifically, the median size for equity crowdfunded deals in 2012 was $190,000 and for debt-crowdfunded deals this figure was $4,700 per deal. To date, the most active segments of this market worldwide are :Arts (all types) 27.7 percent; Social Causes 27.4 percent; Business and Entrepreneurship 16.9 percent; and Energy and Environment 5.9 percent according to Massolution (2013CF The Crowdfunding Industry Report).

Role of Crowdfunding Associations

Most economies where crowdfunding exists have professionally organized crowdfunding associations and networks to coordinate the activities of members, enforce best practices and codes of conduct and represent the interests of investors and entrepreneurs. Crowdfunding associations also provide advocacy, education and support, help develop professional standards, and provide industry research and professional networking opportunities. These associations often partner with industry groups, government, academia and other business associations and affiliates to create a strong and vibrant crowdfunding industry. The National Crowdfunding Association of Canada, National Crowdfunding Association of USA, UK Crowdfunding Association, European crowdfunding network and Israel Crowdfunding Association are some of the active associations operating around the world today.

Regulation

As with any industry that handles people's money, crowd-funding is governed by laws, rules and regulations to protect retail investors who may lack the knowledge, experience and resources to cope with potential significant losses. At the same time, these laws and regulations promote effective competition in the interests of consumers. Regulation is still evolving in most jurisdictions.

In Europe, crowdfunding is largely regulated by national laws, as most platforms circumnavigate pan-European legislation due to the high administrative and financial costs involved. Thus, in practice, 28 different legal frameworks for crowdfunding coexist in this single market. For instance, at the time of writing, the Italian financial regulation authority CONSOB has introduced specific equity crowdfunding laws in Italy, but other countries such as Germany, Austria, and the Netherlands are yet to finalize and put in place the necessary rules and regulation to protect stakeholders and reduce risk in the industry.

In the UK, the Financial Conduct Authority (FCA) published Policy Statement 14/4 in March 2014 outlining the FCA's final rules on the regulation of crowdfunding peer-to-peer lending platforms or peer-to-business lending platforms (on which consumers are able to lend money to individuals or businesses). The FCA also outlined rules for loan-based crowdfunding platforms and investment-based platforms (on which consumers purchase shares or debt securities in new or established businesses, generally structured as UK private limited companies). FCA-regulated firms in the UK include Crowdcube, Seedrs, Abundance Generation, Crowdbnk and Trillion Fund. Being regulated means, among other things, that there is an official complaints channel through which these companies can be held legally responsible for any wrongdoing.

In the United States, on the other hand, the Jumpstart Our Business Startups (JOBS) Act, signed into effect in April 2012, includes crowdfunding provisions designed to make it easier for entrepreneurs to raise funds and get new businesses established before they have to deal with any compliance requirements. In October 2013, the Securities and Exchange Commission (SEC) issued a 585-page set of proposed rules for regulating crowdfunding. The SEC document included an explanation of the rules and the feedback received from stakeholders.

Crowdfunding rules and regulations are generally designed to help ensure that marketing is fair and not misleading, risks are highlighted and minimized and clients' money is protected. They usually provide guidelines on topics such as who can invest and how much can they invest, who can raise money and how much they can raise over what time period, cancellation rights, reporting requirements and dispute resolution.

How to Access Funds through Crowdfunding Platforms

To successfully raise funds to finance your business via a crowdfunding platform requires planning and preparation before ever uploading your online investment profile. Once your campaign is online, managing it effectively will make all the difference to achieving your business financing goals.

Planning and Preparation

- Begin by researching which crowdfunding platform will be best for your specific kind of business, the kind of funding you prefer (debt or equity) and your fundraising goals. You can opt to create a campaign site of your own with crowdfunding and payment tools or register on an appropriate crowdfunding site or online platform.

- Check out the guidelines for the different crowdfunding platforms so you understand their specific requirements, the costs involved in setting up a campaign and the timelines you'll need to follow.

- Plan how you will protect any original ideas that you plan to include in your campaign. *Caution: because most crowdfunding platforms do not have a system or mechanism in place to protect ideas, entrepreneurs are strongly advised to protect their ideas through early filing of patent applications, use of copyright and trademark protections, and use of the recently introduced "Creative Barcode" for protecting ideas supported by the World Intellectual Property Organization.*

■ Clearly establish what your project and campaign is all about and why people will want to support your cause. Set clear, concrete and specific goals and objectives that potential funders and partners can easily understand and relate to. Funders must feel a sense of ownership and have a sense that the final product they're funding is in sight.

■ Have a funding target for each objective. These targets need to be realistic and contribute toward the realization of the primary goals of the business. However, be mindful not to set your overall target too high because with most platforms you only get the money raised if you reach your goal. If you feel your overall target is too high and may be difficult to reach, consider breaking it into project rounds that are more reasonable to achieve. A good financial plan as part of your business plan will help you ascertain the right figures.

■ A funding target should also help you identify which type of crowdfunding platform, as explained previously, will be best suited to your aims.

■ Identify your target audience. Your business goal has to appeal to a certain community or demographic to be successful. If you make it too general, you risk losing out.

■ You must create a range of amounts that people can donate to be part of the project. These can range from as low as $5 to the highest possible amounts, with a large number at the lower-end level to make it easier for people to contribute.

- The rewards you are offering must be clearly stated and tempting to your target audience. Depending on the type of campaign, you could potentially have different rewards based on amounts contributed. Crowdfunding for debt financing, for instance, should offer competitive interest rates to win over investors.

- You will have to prepare a pitch in which your potential backers can read (or watch via a video pitch) and clearly understand why you are running the campaign, who it is for and when it will start. Transparency and honesty about your costs, forecasts, budgets, workflow and operations is extremely important. Of course these also need to be realistic and achievable.

- Most platforms also demand that you make a video about you, your business and your product or project to help potential funders assess the funding opportunity. This video pitch should be brief and not loaded down with too many details. Details and supporting documents can be provided via your website.

- You must also have available well-designed, attention-grabbing promotional materials with photos and illustrations of the project to date and those already involved with the project or supporting the campaign.

- It is equally important to create a buzz before the launch of the campaign. An online buzz through various social media platforms, a pre-launch party where you share flyers and other promotional materials or a giveaway can enhance your chances of having a successful campaign.

- Make time to update, build and strengthen your own database (clients and potential customers) as well as build and strengthen partnerships with your network and those who work with similar target audiences. It's great if you can involve members of your network in some capacity and ask them to help promote the campaign to enable you to expand your reach.

- Before going online, it is essential to have specific marketing and communication plans in place to manage tasks, responsibilities of your team, media requests, and events to help you create a buzz about your campaign. Most importantly, be prepared to communicate intensively with "the crowd" and your network, ready to clarify issues, answer queries and listen to any suggestions and feedback. It is also important to have a system in place to keep the crowd posted on the progress of the project via regular video and email updates. Just be mindful not to become a nuisance by bombarding them.

Launching and Managing Your Campaign

Once you have everything in place behind the scenes, it's time to launch your campaign and start the management process.

- Complete and upload your online investment profile to the site. *(Before doing this, please see the warning about protecting your ideas in the previous section and be sure you have taken all necessary steps to legally protect any original ideas that you plan to include in your profile or campaign.)*

- Once your profile is uploaded, it is time to be on hand with your team to engage with the crowd and potential funders. You'll want to continue creating buzz, answer questions, listen to feedback and monitor and share progress updates. Realize that this level of involvement and interaction needs to continue throughout the campaign even though the initial excitement may have faded for you or your team. Remember that potential investors may not hear about or come across your campaign until late in the process but they'll need to feel that you're as interested in them as you were in the first person to respond to your campaign.

- After your funding target is reached and you've been able to launch your project or start production at last, it is still important to keep your funders involved. They become your most valuable clients and need to have a sense of ownership in the progress of the business.

- If you're unable to reach your target and have to cancel the campaign, it is important to inform your backers, be honest about the situation and update them on your next step. Because they have become an involved support network with you and your project, some funders may even be willing to top up the funding themselves or through their network to help you reach your funding target, or they might know another way to get your venture started.

In some instances, crowdfunding campaigns may not meet their funding target or may take too long to reach their funding target, wiping away any gains if a campaign was aimed toward a project or opportunity with time limitations. Crowdfunding platforms offer a unique opportunity for ongoing engagement with the crowd even after a campaign has been completed or cancelled, giving you the rare opportunity to continue to convince them of your business's prospects, you and your team's strengths and the market opportunity available to investors.

What Investors Look For In a Campaign

Finally let's consider some of the essential considerations that inform investor decisions in backing a crowdfunding campaign. These considerations overlap with those of other types of investors, of course, but with a few important distinctions for crowdfunding.

- Investors are attracted to entrepreneurs who know what they are doing. In-depth research is the only way to prepare adequately for your campaign, ready to handle effectively any questions from the 'crowd' of potential investors. In preparation to launch a campaign, make it a point to anticipate questions that investors could ask and include the answers in your pitch. That puts you ahead and showcases you as a well-informed business person.

- A successful campaign is a product of a well-crafted and effectively delivered pitch. It is the only way to communicate the unique potential of you, your business and your vision to the audience; which only you can do and must endeavor to do exceptionally well.

- Having professional investors such as angel investors on board adds a significant amount of weight and credibility to your campaign which in turn gives retail investors greater confidence in the opportunity.

- It is also important to be transparent and honest at all times as you interact with the audience and respond to their queries.

- Your passion about the project, venture or idea must be unquestionable at all times. And this must also come across in your interaction with "the crowd".

- Most investors are more inclined to take an interest in a campaign and invest when they see others investing in it. Engaging your immediate network of family and friends to invest can give your campaign the necessary boost to make it attractive for others.

- Investors also consider tax breaks in choosing investments. In the UK, for instance, startups registered with Seed Enterprise Investment Scheme (SEIS) and Enterprise Investment Scheme (EIS) tend to be favored over nonregistered ones by some investors. The fact that the startups are registered allows investors to claim up to 50 percent of their original investment on their income tax, or more if the startup fails, and there are no capital gains taxes if the venture is a success.

- You and your team will be expected to make time and be ready to respond to any questions from potential investors either on the platform or other communication mediums set up by you and your team.

■ Most investors also review the Q&A section of entre-preneurs' websites and their video pitches to help them better understand the business. In some cases, potential investors want to post direct questions or personally engage the entrepreneur to clarify any issues they may have. Your ability to keep tabs on all of your business portals and convincingly answer questions and provide adequate information is the key to winning investor support.

Using the Internet and crowdfunding platforms to raise business funds is quite new and still evolving. It is expect-ed that as the industry continues to grow, different types of crowdfunding platforms will continue to be rolled out in coming years to meet the increasing need for new funding sources. Barry James, founder of The Crowd Data Centre, is quoted on the Independent.co.uk website as saying, *"The industry is growing at 10 times the rate of Moore's Law of computing power that has revolutionized business and society."*

The introduction of regulation is expected to help minimize the risk associated with tapping into these platforms to raise much-needed financing by entrepreneurs and small business owners. As Julia Groves, chairman of the UK Crowdfunding Association told Thisismoney.co.uk, *"Regulation will mean a higher level of protection for investors because an independ-ent body will be checking that everybody is doing what they should."* This should also be welcome news for less-sophis-ticated investors who are gaining interest in these platforms but don't have the skills to fully evaluate each campaign to assess their viability.

See Appendix C for a list of some of the established crowdfunding platforms and organizations around the world.

CHAPTER 11

GRANTS

A grant is a non-repayable fund given by a government, foundation or trust to new or existing businesses for specific projects or purpose. Some government agencies fund new projects, such as moving into export for existing businesses.

Across the various schemes in the UK for instance, there is £5bn worth of development capital available annually. Recipients of grants generally do not have to repay or give up a share of their business. Typically a grant only covers between 15-50 percent of the total cost of a business or project.

On the UK grant database alone there are more than 1,500 UK business grant schemes including those from the Government, the EU, Regional Development Agencies, local authorities, Chambers of Commerce and County Enterprise Boards.

The focus and emphasis of grant bodies can be different from nation to nation. For instance, the SBA (Small Business Administration, USA) does not provide direct grants for starting and expanding a business but offers grants to non-profits and educational organizations, some of which help small businesses. On the other hand, "grant aid" is available to UK firms, regulated through EU "state aid" legislation, which allows the UK government to support certain types of businesses and activity.

Discretionary grants are available for some new, small and medium sized businesses usually in specific industry sectors or geographic areas. Some grants offer financial assistance while others offer free or subsidized services ranging from advice, guidance, information services, training and in some cases practical involvement with projects. In most economies, while many schemes are available nationally, each with their own set of criteria, some are targeted locally through local councils, state level governments, provincial governments and municipal assemblies around the world.

Grants are mostly awarded for specific purposes and are usually for proposed projects, selected industry sectors, or geographic areas and require some level of compliance and reporting. Specified purposes may include starting up a new business or opening a branch in an area that needs economic regeneration, researching new products or website development. Some grants require the entrepreneur or business to match the funds to be awarded and reach certain milestones to qualify for support. Depending on location, type of business and what the funds are needed for, an entrepreneur may be eligible for a number of different grants.

The need for governments and organizations to support and promote entrepreneurship and small business development has never been greater. Creating the enabling environment for businesses to thrive has risen to the forefront of the agenda of many governments and organizations around the globe. The aftermath of the 2008 financial crisis left a lot of businesses in a dire financial state; with the subsequent drying up of traditional sources of funding and the cautionary stance of investors, governments were forced to step in and offer much needed support to businesses, especially small businesses, to help them grow and shore up the spiraling unemployment rates.

Grant schemes and initiatives are designed to encourage new and growing businesses, to create wealth and ultimately create jobs. Although a number of private foundations such as Ewing Marion Kauffman Foundation in the US (they do not make grants directly to individuals but invest in partner organizations with shared vision and passion for education and entrepreneurship) and the Prince's Trust in the UK also support enterprise, governments are the major grant providers in most nations. To help achieve this, they usually set aside a portion of taxpayers' money – as small business grants - through a variety of departments, agencies, ministries, other local government bodies and schemes to encourage and support enterprise development.

Most businesses are eligible at any one time to apply for a number of different business startup grants and support schemes which are distributed in a wide variety of forms. However, the process can be quite daunting for the entrepreneur seeking to access these grants. The argument for the lengthy and cumbersome process has always been that these are taxpayer funds and must be carefully managed and accounted for.

Types of Grants

Grants come in different forms other than cash. Below are some of the main types for consideration.

Direct Grant

A direct grant is often given as a cash award for activities such as training, employment, export development, recruitment and capital investment projects. Most schemes usually require the company involved to match the grant up to 50 percent of the cost in some cases. In the UK for instance, there are about 300 direct grant agencies listed on the government Business Finance Support finder website which also features local grant providers under the government's £3.2bn Regional Growth Fund. On the other hand, as stated previously, the Small Business Administration (USA) does not provide direct grants for businesses.

Soft Loan

This is a type of grant where businesses are offered loans with significantly better or more flexible terms. The terms and conditions of repayment are more generous (or softer) than they would be under normal prevailing market conditions. For instance, there may be long moratorium periods allowed, significantly lower interest rates, or no interest to be paid at all, longer repayment periods, no collateral to secure the loan and many other "soft" terms. Start Up Loans, a Government-funded scheme in the UK, which offers new business loans up to £25,000 with 12 months moratorium is an example. There are a number of other organizations that offer soft loans and guarantees. Social enterprises or charities can also access soft loans from such organizations as Big Issue Invest, the investment arm of the Big Issue which has soft loans from £50,000 to £1m available for positive impact, socially-driven entrepreneurs and also operates "participation loans" where repayment is linked to future performance of the enterprise.

The Prince's Trust provides soft loans of up to £4,000, as well as advisory support for young entrepreneurs aged between 18 – 30 years, with interest capped at 3 percent and repayments spread over a period of 2 -5 years. The Small Business Administration (US) has a number of loan programs such as General Small Business loans (which includes financial help for businesses with special requirements), the Microloan program (which provides small short term loans - up to $35,000 - to small businesses for working capital or the purchase of inventory, supplies, furniture, fixtures, machinery and/or equipment) and Disaster loans (which provides low-interest loans to homeowners, renters, businesses of all sizes, and most private non-profit organizations).

Loan Guarantees

Under the loan guarantee scheme option, a business can get a third party to guarantee a loan. For instance, in the UK if an entrepreneur has no security, the government's Small Firms Loan Guarantee guarantees 75 percent of the loan in return for an annual premium of 2 percent. UK businesses that have an annual turnover under £5.6m and are less than 5 years old are eligible for this scheme. In the US, banks and other lending institutions offer a number of Small Business Administration guaranteed programs to assist small businesses, such as the Export Loan Programs, Express Programs, Special Purpose Loans Program and Rural Lender Advantage program.

Equity Finance

This is a scheme where a capital sum is injected into the business and the provider of the funds takes an equity share of the enterprise. As with other equity funding options mentioned previously, when the value of the firm increases the invested amount can then be returned. The difference here is that the expectations and requirements of the providers of public funds are usually less demanding, unlike others such as venture capitalists.

Under schemes such as the UK government's Enterprise Investment Scheme (EIS) and Seed Enterprise Investment

Scheme (SEIS), businesses are helped to raise finance by providing tax relief to investors who buy a share in a business.

Subsidised or Free Business Consultation

These are schemes aimed at offering subsidised or free independent advisory services to entrepreneurs to help them navigate the start-up processes through 'Business Hotline' and face-to-face meetings with Business Support Officers. These services also tend to include help to assess entrepreneur's skills and competencies in business management, financial management, bookkeeping and other basic business skills. The Welsh Assembly government in Wales-UK, for instance, offers free independent advice on starting a business and operates an instant hotline for business queries from entre-preneurs, small business owners and aspiring entrepreneurs, through its Business Support Service unit.

Training & Network Support

Business consultation is often followed by training in those areas where entrepreneurs lack the requisite skills and competencies for managing their own businesses. This particular scheme is commonly offered by most grant bodies on the assumption that entrepreneurs are better served to run a business successfully if they have the necessary skills and knowledge to drive the business forward. Also, with the high failure rates among startups it is seen as one of the best ways to help entrepreneurs succeed and not become part of the failure statistics. Some government schemes take training even further by setting up business support network programs through which training seminars are delivered on legislation, best practices and other elements that are vital to the successful running of a business.

Resource Facilities

Other initiatives such as incubator and accelerator schemes offer access to publicly owned facilities for use at subsidised rates or at no charge. These include hot desking space, internet access, telephone facilities, meeting rooms as well as workshop spaces for startups and small businesses. Most local government business development centers make these resources and facilities available to help budding entrepreneurs to find their feet.

Research Cost Sharing

Research and development plays a major role in the growth of companies. However, the costs involved can prevent small firms from embarking on meaningful research projects. There are grants and schemes available that enable these costs to be subsidised or shared with other businesses; the outcomes and expertise gained are then shared among the network or participants. In the US, for example, if a small business is engaged in scientific research and development it may qualify for federal grants under the Small Business Innovation Research (SBIR) and the Small Business Technology Transfer (STTR) programs. These programs are designed to encourage small businesses to undertake research and development projects that meet federal R&D objectives and have high potential for commercialization.

Other Allowances

A business could also be eligible for other government schemes, such as tax allowances for new businesses, including capital allowances for investment in equipment and premises (so you can deduct a proportion of these costs from your taxable profits over several years) and stamp duty relief in disadvantaged areas in the UK. Tax credits and tax allowances may also be available for businesses to research, develop new products, processes or services.

The best way to find relevant funding to suit a business need is to visit local government websites or offices and speak with business or enterprise development units or departments to help identify schemes that match your need as an entrepreneur.

In the UK, for instance, your local Business Link office can help you identify relevant European, national and local grant schemes and will contact them to check your eligibility and in the US the Small Business Association website is a great way to start. You should also check participating banks and other financial institutions about SBA guaranteed loans, or contact state level enterprise offices to check your eligibility for any available grant support schemes.

The application process for a grant can be lengthy and may be unsuccessful:

- if the business plan is unrealistic;

- if there are no matched funds from the applicant;

- or if it's unclear how important the funds are to the project's success.

If you spend time and effort applying for grants, it is important to do your homework thoroughly and to exercise patience because grants do take time to come through should an application be successful. It is important to also note that with a significant number of schemes you may not be reimbursed for payments you made before the commencement of the project.

Before you apply, you'll need to provide the following:

- the project's details and its potential benefits;

- a comprehensive business plan with full costings;

- the entrepreneur's experience as well that of key managers relevant to the project.

Proposals are often assessed on their relevance to a grant's aim, the expertise of the management and their approach to execution.

From the above, we have identified a number of the major funding options available to you as an entrepreneur, startup or small business owner.

Evolving Funding Options

It is also true to say that as business evolves there will be a never-ending cycle of funding options that can be sought, especially as technology advances. One such recent addition to the options available is the PayPal Working Capital loan program, launched in September 2013 in the US and expanded into the UK in August 2014. According to information on the website Paypal.com, "PayPal Working Capital gives businesses access to the capital they need, but it's faster and easier than traditional loans. It's available to select businesses that already process payments through PayPal...PayPal Working Capital is a loan of a fixed amount, with a single fixed fee. There are no due dates, minimum monthly payments, periodic interest charges, late fees, pre-payment fees, penalty fees, or any other fees." Another such example is Virgin StartUp, the not-for-profit Virgin company that provides funding (Virgin StartUp Loan) ranging from £500-£25,000 together with mentoring to entrepreneurs looking to get their business started.

To position yourself to access any form of funding or to attract the right kind of investment, however, you must always ensure the fundamentals are in place, such as, what the funds are for, how much is needed and what is the business proposition. This can only be clearly assessed and articulated with a well-researched and well written business plan.

In the next chapter we will walk-through what the business plan is all about, what it can do for you and your business and how to create one by yourself, if you choose to, instead of getting help from a professional.

If you already have a good business plan you may want to skip to **Part 4 — Master-Class Pitching Techniques.**

PART 3

CREATING A COMPELLING
BUSINESS PLAN

CHAPTER 12

What Is Your Plan?

*"By failing to prepare,
you are preparing to fail."*

Benjamin Franklin, (late)
One of the Founding
Fathers of the United States

Planning for your business is a luxury you can't do without as an entrepreneur or business owner. Any business – startup or existing business - aiming to become a sustainable success should have a realistic business plan regardless of whether you're using it to raise finance from banks, friends and family, angel investors, VCs, grant bodies or even investing your own money. It is a fact of business that NO serious investor will give money to an entrepreneur without a PLAN for the Business.

Given the focus of this book – pitching to win investor support for business success – a good business plan is the basis and platform from which a winning pitch can be developed and "sold" to an investor. Although an entrepreneur may not need to use the whole plan in any given pitch session, the chapters in this part of the book will help you to structure and clearly outline your business goals, proposition and prospects so that you can develop a master-class pitch to win investor backing and cash investment.

The greatest benefit of the planning process lies in researching and thinking about your business in a systematic way. This process helps you to think things through thoroughly, to study and research if you are not sure of the facts, and to look at your ideas critically. An international consultant, Dr. Graeme Edwards, once said, *"It's not the plan that is important, it's the planning."* In other words, it's the "process" that offers the business owner the best shot at mapping out the best way forward.

A good plan can have many other benefits.

- It gives you and your potential partners and investors a clear sense of direction, telling you where you're going and how you're going to get there.

- It becomes a blueprint by which management and employees can fully understand and appreciate what the ultimate aim and vision of the founders are and how to contribute towards it.

- It helps you to prioritize and keep track of what needs to happen in what order to achieve maximum success.

- It is also a vital document when you're looking for funding – without a business plan you can't adequately assess your needs and convince potential lenders that your business proposal is achievable.

- It gives you something concrete against which you can measure your progress, keeping your company on track and in some cases it can help you avoid expanding too quickly which can have disastrous consequences for a small business.

■ According to a recent research by Lloyds TSB, UK, "Having a business plan can help increase your profits. Companies that undertake regular business planning have an average profit margin of 54 percent, and those that don't, average 35 percent."

That said, I've come to appreciate why many aspiring entrepreneurs and business owners seem either intimidated by a business plan, question its importance or never bother about it at all. Whatever the challenge is, the benefits of a business plan to the success of a business far outweigh not having one because it is a document that helps you to: articulate and clearly put together your ideas and research into a more structured format; clarify the purpose of the business; verify that the business idea is realistic and commercially viable; help set sales and financial targets; plan for the future of the business; and set out the business and marketing strategies, all of which are essential to help you to answer any investor questions and equip you to pitch your business well enough to win investor support.

A business plan has both internal and external uses. For internal purposes:

- it can be used to help measure success;

- it can help you to focus on development efforts;

- it can help you to spot potential pitfalls before they manifest;

- and it can help you to structure the financial aspects of a business.

On the other hand, it is used externally to:

- introduce the business to, or apply for funding, from bankers, external investors (friends, angel investors, VCs), grant providers;

- introduce the business to potential buyers;

- and attract potential partners.

Whichever way you look at it, the business plan is simply one of the most essential pieces of documentation that any person starting a business needs to put together.

In the words of Chris Corrigan, an Australian businessman, *"You can't overestimate the need to plan and prepare. In most of the mistakes I've made, there has been this common theme of inadequate planning beforehand. You really can't over-prepare in business!"*

Ultimately the business plan is the best possible way to address all aspects of your business and must be comprehensive enough to help answer the following questions:

- What are the objectives for my business?

- How will I achieve these objectives?

- What are the risks involved?

- What is the timescale for major milestones?

- How much will it cost?

- Who are the key members of the management team?

- What products and services am I offering and what problems do they solve?

■ What is the market size, who are the customers, competitors and what are the sales projections?

Planning is key in ensuring the continuous existence of a business. Every business that seeks to be successful must have a business plan and must regularly review it to ensure it continues to meet its needs. It is also sensible to review current performance on a regular basis and to identify the most likely strategies for growth. Once you have reviewed your progress and identified the key growth areas that you want to target, it's time to revisit your business plan and make it a road map for the next stages of your business.

For a new business, it is important to establish the purpose of the plan from the onset because the emphasis of any plan should be dependent on the intended user. In the next few chapters, we will discuss the essential components of a typical business plan.

CHAPTER 13

THE EXECUTIVE SUMMARY

The executive summary is an overview of the business or summary of the business plan and a synopsis of the key points of your entire plan. It should include highlights from each section of the document from the key features of the business opportunity to elements of the financial forecasts. It should clearly and concisely address the following.

Overview of the company.

- Recap of the opportunity. Quantify and describe the opportunity and where you fit. Explain why you are in business along with the reasons you will be able to take advantage of this opportunity.

- Brief summary of the market. How large is the market and what stage of development is it in (early growth versus mature)? What are the key drivers, trends, and influences in the market?

- Differentiation. What separates you from the rest of the pack – what is your USP (Unique Selling Point)? Is your product proprietary, patented, copyrighted?

- Is your service or product better/faster/cheaper and, if so, why? Is your advantage a temporary opportunity, and are there steps you can take to protect your position?

- Description of products or services. A very brief overview and description of your products and services.

- Management composition. It is said that investors invest in people not products. It's a proven fact that a company's management team is one of the best predictors of success and investors will look very closely at the individuals who will be managing the company. The ideal scenario is that senior managers have previously started and successfully managed companies in the same type of business. If not, you need to emphasize the next point.

- Relevant experience of the management team. Names of companies and positions held and milestones achieved are worth emphasizing.

- Nature and use of proceeds. What type of funding are you looking for? Equity capital, grants, or loans? Undercapitalization is a major cause of new startup business failure. You should have a very clear idea of how much money you will need to operate your business for the first full year. Bank loan officers and investors always want to know how the funds will be used.

- Key financials, such as forecasts, sales, cash flow statement and profit and loss account and balance sheet.

The ultimate purpose of the executive summary is to help you succinctly explain the basics of your business in a way that both informs and interests the reader. It should be concise, no longer than two pages, and interesting.

CHAPTER 13: THE EXECUTIVE SUMMARY

Your pitch in any given scenario should capture the key points from the executive summary and be delivered in a way to win over an investor or partner. If, after reading the executive summary, an investor or an evaluation manager understands what the business is about and is keen to know more, it has done its job.

CHAPTER 14

GENERAL PERSONAL AND COMPANY DESCRIPTION

Personal details. Name, home address, contact details (telephone, mobile phone, email), date of birth, and marital status.

Business details. Business name, business address, telephone, e-mail and website. Social media details such as Twitter and LinkedIn links.

Mission statement. Many companies have a brief mission statement, usually 30 words or fewer, explaining their reasons for being and their guiding principles. If you want to draft a mission statement this is a good place to put it in the plan.

Company goals and objectives. Goals are destinations. Objectives are progress markers along the way to goal achievement.

Business philosophy. What is important to you in business?

To whom will you market your products? State it briefly here—it will be dealt with more thoroughly in the Marketing Plan section.

Describe your industry. Is it a growth industry? What changes do you foresee in the industry, short term, medium term and long term? How will your company be poised to take advantage of them?

Describe your most important company strengths and core competencies. What factors will make the company succeed?

What do you think your major competitive strengths are? What background experience, skills, and strengths do you personally bring to this new venture?

Legal form of ownership. Sole proprietor, partnership, corporation, Limited Liability Company, social enterprise or charitable organization? Why have you selected this form?

Exit strategy. You may want to explain to investors how they will get their money back, what you are anticipating they will recover in excess of their investment, and in what time frame. Possible exit strategies can include the sale or merger of your company, a management buyout, an IPO, or a private placement.

CHAPTER 15

PRODUCTS AND SERVICES

Describe in depth your products or services with:

- technical specifications;
- drawings;
- photographs;
- sales brochures;
- other bulky items belong in Appendices.

You must also discuss:

- pricing;
- service;
- support;
- warranty;
- production, etc.

What are the advantages of your products or services, and how do they compare to the competition? Examples include level of quality or unique or distinguishing features.

Have they been trademarked, patented or any such intellectual property rights secured, if they must.

What is the timetable for introducing these products, and what steps need to be taken to ensure that this timeline is met?

Are there other vendors involved, and if so, who are they and where do they fit?

Have your products been tested or evaluated, and if so, where, when, and what were the results?

Are there plans for future or next-generation products, and if so, what are they and when will they be available?

Are these new products included in your revenue and cost projections?

In-depth knowledge of your products and services is essential, without this information you have no business. Your ability to answer the above questions will enable you to clearly describe them and better answer any potential questions that may come up at any pitch session.

CHAPTER 16
MARKETING PLAN

RESEARCH

Why? It is quite deceptive to assume that you already know about your intended market. You need to do market research to make sure you are on track. Use the opportunity to uncover data and to question your marketing efforts.

How? There are two kinds of market research: primary and secondary.

Primary research means gathering your own data.

Secondary research means using published information, such as industry profiles, trade journals, newspapers, magazines, census data, demographic profiles, business and other research reports. This type of information is available from public libraries, industry associations, chambers of commerce, vendors who sell to your industry, and from government agencies.

In your marketing plan, be as specific as possible: give statistics, numbers, and sources. The marketing plan will be the basis later on of all important sales projections.

Facts about your industry:

- What is the total size of your market?

- What percentage share of the market will you have?

- What is the current demand in your target market?

- What are the trends in your target market—growth trends, trends in consumer preferences, and trends in product development?

- What is the growth potential and opportunity for a business of your size?

What barriers to entry do you face in entering this market with your new company? Some typical barriers may include:

- high capital costs;
- high production costs;
- high marketing costs;
- consumer acceptance and brand recognition;
- training and skills;
- unique technology and patents;
- trade unions;
- shipping costs;
- tariff barriers and quotas.

How will you overcome the barriers? How could the following affect your company?

- Change in technology?
- Change in government regulations?
- Change in the economy?
- Change in your industry?

PRODUCTS

In the *Products and Services* section of your business plan you described your products and services. Now, describe them from your customers' point of view.

Features and benefits. List all of your major products or services. For each product or service:

- Describe the most important features. What is special about it?

- Describe the benefits. That is, what will the product do for the customer?

Note the difference between features and benefits, and think about them. For example, a house that gives shelter and lasts a long time is made with certain materials and to a certain design; those are its features. Its benefits include pride of ownership, financial security, providing for the family, and inclusion in a neighborhood. You build features into your product so that you can sell the benefits.

What after-sale services will you provide? Some examples are delivery, warranty, service contracts, support, follow-up, and refunds.

CUSTOMERS

Identify your targeted customers, their characteristics, and their geographic locations, i.e. their demographics. The description will be completely different depending on whether you plan to sell to other businesses or directly to consumers. Then, for each customer group, construct what is called a demographic profile, including age, gender, location, income level, social class, occupation, and education level. For business customers, the demographic factors might be industry, location, size of firm, quality, technology, and price preferences.

COMPETITION

What products and companies will compete with yours? List your major competitors (names and addresses). Will they compete with you across the board or just for certain products, certain customers, or in certain locations?

Will you have important indirect competitors? For example, video rental stores compete with theaters although they are different types of businesses. How will your products or services compare with the competition?

Other areas to consider: niche, marketing strategy, promotion, promotional budget, pricing (explain your methods of setting prices), proposed location, and distribution channels (how you sell your products or services: retail, direct - mail order, web, catalogue; wholesale, your own sales force, agents, independent representatives, bid on contracts).

SALES FORECAST

It's time to attach some numbers to your plan. Use a sales forecast spreadsheet to prepare a month-by-month projection. The forecast should be based on your historical sales, the marketing strategies that you have just described in your market research, and industry data, if available.

You may want to do two forecasts:

1) A "best guess," which is what you really expect to happen.

2) A "worst case" low estimate that you are confident you can reach no matter what happens.

Remember to keep notes on your research and your assumptions as you build this sales forecast and all subsequent spreadsheets in the plan. This is critical if you are going to present it to funding sources. These notes will help you to remember the underlining assumptions behind your projections and strategy.

CHAPTER 17
SWOT ANALYSIS

A SWOT analysis simply helps you to assess your *Strengths* and *Weaknesses*, and the *Opportunities* and *Threats* your business faces or may face in the course of operations. It provides a clear basis for examining your business performance and prospects.

There are various ways to assess your *Strengths*. Continual dialogue with customers or potential customers and suppliers may provide a clue as to where your strengths lie. Rising sales, for an existing business, in a particular product; a strong balance sheet; positive cash flow; growing turnover and profitability; skilled financial management; skilled employees; successful recruitment; effective training and development; modern, low-cost production facilities; a good location; market leadership in a profitable niche; an established customer base; a strong product range; effective research and development; a skilled sales team; and thorough after-sales service are all good indicators.

Weaknesses, on the other hand, can be identified through various indicators, most of which are the opposite of the strength of the business. They are usually known but tend to be ignored. For example, not having the right financial management expert or system in place will result in poor credit control, leading to unpredictable cash flow or insufficient funds available for investment. Other weaknesses may be a limited or outdated product range; complacency and failure to innovate; over-reliance on a small number of customers;

expertise and control locked up in a few key personnel; high staff turnover; long leases tying the business to unsuitable premises or equipment; inefficient processes; outdated equipment; high cost of production; and low productivity.

Changes in the business's external environment can provide great *Opportunities*, which, when well-managed, can be turned into an advantage for the business. External factors include things such as improved access to potential new customers and markets overseas; the development of new distribution channels such as the Internet; deterioration in a competitor's performance or the insolvency of a competitor; securing financiers to fund expansion, which could be as a result of political, legislative, or regulatory change; economic trends such as a fall in interest rates; introduction of new process technology; increased sales to existing customers or new leads gained through them; and social developments such as demographic changes.

Threats can be major or minor. Minor threats can equally affect your business and have far-reaching consequences, destroying its survival and profitability. Threats can be in the form of loss of a significant customer; price rises from suppliers; lenders reducing credit lines or increasing charges; improved competitive products or the emergence of new competitors; key personnel leaving, perhaps with trade secrets; new technology that makes your products obsolete or gives competitors an advantage; legal action taken against you by a customer; social developments such as consumer demands for environmentally friendly or ethics-based products; political, legislative, and regulatory changes such as new regulations increasing your costs or requiring product redesign.

The results of SWOT analyses should not be the end but rather a starting point. You can capitalize on the results and play to your strengths, as each business is different. Opportunities that are in line with your strengths may prompt you to pursue a strategy of aggressive expansion.

You should prioritize the weaknesses and address those that can be addressed. Weaknesses that cannot be addressed now must be acknowledged and respected until time and resources allow a solution. Some weaknesses can be turned into strengths or opportunities, such as turning a shortage of production capacity into scarcity value for your product. Other weaknesses, such as financial ones, might be solved by raising further funds, or management shortcomings may be solved by recruiting new personnel. Some weaknesses will need a significant investment in time and resources. You may, for instance, need to start a program of improvements through training or quality management. The analysis could also suggest other strategic options for the business, such as taking defensive measures in areas of threat where weakness had been identified or diversifying away from areas of significant threat to more promising opportunities.

Protecting your business against threats may include fostering good employee relations; taking out insurance cover against obvious potential disasters; investing in legal protection for your intellectual property; taking advantage of low fixed interest rates to move your overdraft to long term loans; ensuring you have clear and reasonable contracts with suppliers, customers, and employees; building relationships with suppliers and customers; drawing up realistic contingency plans to cope with potential crises; and introducing the right types of service contracts for key personnel.

Often there is the temptation to highlight all the opportunities and strengths and to ignore or downplay the weaknesses and threats. This is not a good strategy especially when you are to pitch to investors. It is better to appreciate and acknowledge the weaknesses and threats in your pitch. Investors often prefer that and may be more willing to help you manage them than you downplaying their existence or impact. Being honest in your weaknesses and the potential threats you face is considered a virtue and can earn you more favor. Of course, you must have also done your best to think through any possible ways you could address weaknesses and threats and be able to present them, when asked, even if they are not concrete or fully researched.

CHAPTER 18
OPERATIONAL PLAN

Explain the daily operation of the business, its location, equipment, people, processes, and surrounding environment.

Production. How and where are your products or services produced?

Location. What qualities do you need in a location? Describe the type of location you'll have.

Legal environment. Licensing requirements, permits, health and safety requirements, workplace or environmental regulations, special regulations covering your industry or profession, etc.

Personnel. Number of employees, type of labor, where you find the right employees, quality of existing staff, pay structure, training methods and requirements, task breakdown, etc.

Inventory. What kind of inventory will you keep: raw materials, supplies, finished goods? Average value in stock (i.e. what is your inventory investment)? Rate of turnover and how this compares to the industry averages. Seasonal buildups. Lead time for ordering.

Suppliers Identify key suppliers, with names and addresses, type and amount of inventory furnished, credit and delivery policies, history, and reliability.

Credit policies. Do you plan to sell on credit? Do you really need to sell on credit? Is it customary in your industry and expected by your clientele? If yes, what policies will you have about who gets credit and how much? How will you check the credit worthiness of new applicants? What terms will you offer your customer--that is, how much credit, and when will payment be due?

Managing your accounts receivable. If you do extend credit, you should do an aging report, i.e. a list of customers' accounts receivable by how long they are owing which will alert management to any slow paying customers at least monthly so that you can track how much of your money is tied up in credit given to customers and alert you to slow payment problems.

Managing your accounts payable. You should also age your accounts payable (the amount you owe to your suppliers). This helps you plan who to pay and when. Paying too early depletes your cash but paying late can cost you valuable discounts and can damage your credit.

CHAPTER 19

MANAGEMENT AND ORGANIZATION PLAN

The knowledge, caliber and experience of your team is a vital consideration for potential investors assuming you have or are going to need employees to work with from day one. Of course if you work alone, then your skills, qualifications and abilities will be very much scrutinized. You must be able to clearly establish:

- Who will manage the business on a day-to-day basis?

- What experience does that person bring to the business?

- What special or distinctive competencies does he or she have?

- Is there a plan for continuation of the business if this person is lost or incapacitated?

This section should go into some detail about the individuals who will be entrusted with the investor's money. Stress relevant experience and previous successes. This section of the plan should include:

- biographic summary of key management;
- organizational charts (current and future);
- manpower table;
- board of advisors;
- board of directors.

If you'll have more than ten employees, create an organizational chart showing the management hierarchy and who is responsible for key functions. Include position descriptions for key employees. If you are seeking loans or investors, include resumes (in the *Appendices*) of owners and key employees.

Professional and Advisory Support

List the following:

- board of directors;
- management advisory board;
- attorney;
- accountant;
- insurance agent.

Angel investors and VCs may want a place on your board and will also require you to justify who is on your board which means you must seriously consider who gets to be appointed. Avoid appointing people because they are friends, family or people you just like to have around.

CHAPTER 20

Personal Financial Statement

Include personal financial statements for each owner and major stockholder showing assets and liabilities held outside the business and personal net worth. Owners will often have to draw on personal assets to finance the business and these statements will show what is available. Bankers and investors usually want this information as well.

It is also important that thought goes into the amount of money that you require per month to maintain your current standard of living, let alone improve it. The business needs to know how much you require so that pricing decisions can be realistically made.

Start-Up Expenses and Capitalization

For a lot of businesses, you will have quite a number of expenses before you even begin operating your business. It's important to estimate these expenses accurately and then to plan where you will get sufficient capital. Remember, this will include the money for buying or leasing premises, making those premises suitable for your business (even if working from home, you may need to convert a room into an office), any equipment you may need, and working money to get you through those first lean months as the business becomes established.

Some of the quick questions that need to be realistically answered are:

- Where will I get the money that I need to start up my business?

- Do I have money of my own?

- Can my family and friends help me?

- Do I qualify for an existing government grant or scheme?

- Is a loan from the bank my best option?

- Should I seek debt or equity investment from angel investors, venture capitalists or crowdfunding sources?

- How much will the interest rate be?

The more thorough your research efforts, the less chance there is that you will leave out important expenses or under-estimate them. A rule of thumb is that contingencies should equal at least 20 percent of the total of all other start-up expenses.

Explain your research and how you arrived at your forecast of expenses. Give sources, amounts, and terms of proposed loans. Also explain in detail how much will be contributed by each equity investor and what percentage ownership each will have.

Careful consideration must be given to ensure you don't give away too much ownership to reduce your personal drive or offer too little to make your offer less attractive to potential investors, or in the worst case but most common scenario, over value your business.

CHAPTER 21

FINANCIAL PLAN

The financial plan may consist of twelve months' or one to five years' profit and loss projection, a cash flow projection, a projected balance sheet, and a break-even calculation. Together, they constitute a reasonable estimate of your company's financial future. More importantly, the process of thinking through the financial plan will improve your insight into the inner financial workings of your business.

Projected cash flow. If the profit projection is the heart of your business plan, cash flow is the blood. Businesses fail because they cannot pay their bills. Every part of your business plan is important but none of it means a thing if you run out of cash.

Profit and loss statement. The primary tool for good financial reporting is the profit and loss statement. This is a measure of a company's sales and expenses over a specific period of time. It is prepared at regular intervals (monthly for the first year and annually through five years) to show the results of operating during those accounting periods. It should follow generally accepted accounting principles and must contain specific revenue and expense categories regardless of the nature of the business.

Figures such as sales, gross profit, cost of sales, total expenses and net profit/loss are vital when it comes to pitching. You simply cannot deliver an effective pitch without familiarizing yourself and even memorising the figures where necessary, at least for the first five years.

Opening day balance sheet. A balance sheet is one of the fundamental financial reports that a business needs for reporting and for financial management. A balance sheet shows what items of value are held by the company (assets) and what its debts are (liabilities). When liabilities are subtracted from assets, the remainder is owners' equity.

Break-even analysis. A break-even analysis predicts the sales volume, at a given price, required to recover total costs. The sales level is the dividing line between operating at a loss and operating at a profit. Expressed as a formula, break-even is:

$$\text{Break-even Sales} = \frac{\text{Fixed Costs}}{1 - \text{Variable Costs}}$$

Where fixed costs are expressed in dollars, but variable costs are expressed as a percentage of total sales.

Everything you've included in the plan up to this point should support your financial assumptions and projections. In other words, the reader shouldn't be surprised when they see your three- to five-year revenue forecast because you've given them detailed information on the market, the opportunity, and your strategies. You've described the advantages that you have over your competition; you have outlined how you plan to reach the market and the management team that you have to help you achieve your objectives. Your projections should represent a logical conclusion to everything that you've included in the plan.

Some of the supporting documents that can be included in your *Appendices* are:

- brochures and advertising materials;
- industry reports and information;

- forecasted profit and loss statement;
- forecasted cash flow statement;
- blueprints and plans, maps and photos of location;
- magazine articles or other articles;
- detailed lists of equipment owned or to be purchased;
- copies of leases and contracts;
- letters of support from future customers;
- market research studies;
- list of assets available as collateral for a loan
- any other materials needed to support the assumptions in this plan;

It is very important to appreciate the fact that although a good business plan covers all aspects of the business, all of the above will not be applicable to every single business. The content, format and how many sections that are necessary or applicable to your business is determined by:

- the purpose or goal for producing a business plan;
- the audience it is intended for;
- the type or nature of business under consideration;
- the size of the business;
- and the complexities of operating such a business.

For instance, a professional skilled services business may not require the huge capital investment for machinery and stock, or even premises, which a manufacturing or product wholesale or retail business may require upfront. As such, the business plan will be much more straightforward and less detailed for such a service business than a manufacturing or product retail business.

To develop a quality pitch for investors and partners largely depends on the seriousness you attach to the planning and preparation of a business plan as this process gives you the opportunity to realistically and structurally analyse and assess your business proposition and prospects; spot challenges far ahead to enable you adequately respond; and equip you to confidently address any questions that may be thrown at you in a pitching session. How much time and resources you spend on the process is what guarantees your success. The former president of the US, Abraham Lincoln, once said, *"Give me six hours to chop down a tree and I will spend the first four sharpening the axe."* And no matter how lofty or good natured your goals and ideas are, *"A goal without a plan is just a wish."* — Antoine de Saint-Exupéry.

I sincerely believe that, having adequately gone through the above business planning process, you will have the facts, figures and assumptions necessary to craft and deliver a master-class business pitch to win over investors and partners for their cash investment and support. Now it's time to master the techniques to deliver your winning pitch.

PART 4

MASTER-CLASS PITCHING TECHNIQUES

CHAPTER 22

THE PITCHING CHALLENGE

"You can have brilliant ideas, but if you can't get them across, your ideas won't get you anywhere."

Lee Iacocca an American businessman
known for engineering the
Ford Mustang and Ford Pinto cars

In the first chapter I defined pitching as *"the art of making a presentation in person, writing or via video to persuade an individual or audience to support your vision, buy your products or services, or choose you to do a job or invest in your idea or business."*

In subsequent chapters I've established why it is necessary for entrepreneurs and business owners to develop essential pitching skills to position them to take advantage of opportunities when they present themselves.

It also should be perfectly understood that one of the most limiting factors in starting or growing a business is funding. With the funding challenge comes the need to seek investor support to either launch the business or grow an existing one. Your ability to negotiate the interest rate down as much as possible with terms to your advantage can have a significant effect on the overall cost of a bank loan.

Not only that, pitching is also necessary to win over customer business, to negotiate better supplier terms and conditions, and to persuade banks and other debt funding lenders to give their business and support. An entrepreneur's ability to do this right can make a significant difference to the success of the business.

Your ability to negotiate the interest rate down as much as possible with terms to your advantage can have a significant effect on the overall cost of a bank loan.

For many entrepreneurs, however, pitching is the one major thing that does not come naturally, and many would do anything to avoid it or get someone else to deliver it on their behalf. The problem is that there are not many investors willing to listen to anyone other than the entrepreneur make the pitch because it is an important measure of an entrepreneur's understanding of the business, market and how to operate in it. It is also considered a vital art that an entrepreneur must master and employ many times throughout the life of the business to ensure its continued success. An entrepreneur's inability to develop this skill will always mean relying on others to promote and drive the business which is seen as detrimental to the growth and success of the business.

When asked about the challenges they face when it comes to pitching, most entrepreneurs say:

- What should be included in a pitch?

- How long is a pitch?

- What questions are likely to be asked?

- What figures or numbers should I focus on in the pitch?

- Do I talk about me, my business or my plan?

- What type of investor or funding option will best suit my vision or dream for my business?

- How much of the percentage of ownership can I offer to attract an investor?

- Do I deliver with a full PowerPoint- like presentation?

- Do I talk about all my limitations and weaknesses and how will that help me in my bid to get investor cash?

These are only a few of the challenges expressed by entrepreneurs.

In the next section we'll look at
Preparing For The Pitch
— the *first Master-Class Technique* in delivering a perfect pitch.

CHAPTER 23

PREPARING FOR THE PITCH

"Before speaking with investors it's crucial that you're able to articulate certain key areas of your business. What's your business model? What problem are you trying to solve? Who does your company serve? Not only should you be able to painlessly answer these types of questions, you must do so in a way that's clear and concise."

Mark Burnett and **Clay Newbill**,
Executive Producers
of ABC's Shark Tank show

Building your confidence and understanding the workings of your business, industry, competition, market and customers is paramount to the success of your delivery. If you have been through the business plan process effectively most of these areas will have been covered and you will have the facts and figures at hand to be ready for any pitch.

It is important to note that whereas you can be woefully and inade-

It is important to note that whereas you can be woefully and inadequately prepared for a pitch, you can never be over prepared for it.

125

quately prepared for a pitch, you can never be over prepared for it. The following are some of the essential things to consider in your preparation for a pitching session:

I.   Define your vision and goal and understand what the pitch is for. If the pitch is to enable you to win over an investor for funding purposes, then it is important to state what your funding objectives are, which funding option will best suit your business and what you intend to use the funds specifically for in your business. Is it to buy machinery, raw materials, advertising, transport, servers, to hire staff or shore up your working capital or for a project?

In the case of projects, it is equally important to calculate exactly what you need so you must plan the project in phases with achievable milestones and funding requirements for each stage. This will mean raising only as much capital as is necessary to reach your milestones because often investors will only release the funds in tranches or cycles – one stage at a time. The performance of each stage against the target milestones will prompt the release of the next round of funding.

Investors always like to know how their money will help your business and how they will earn profit from their investment.

Investors always like to know how their money will help your business and how they will earn profit from their investment.

II.   Clearly articulate what the product or service is, the problem it solves, the value it brings to your target customers and clients and the benefits to them.

III. Any intellectual property, such as trademark or patent that you may have applied for or secured to protect your idea or inventions. It is important to highlight them in your pitch and to have all necessary supporting documents on hand to show investors. Intellectual property is considered a major asset and carries a lot of weight in an investor's consideration.

IV. Identify the specific customer segments you are targeting and your positioning in that market, how you will serve this customer segment, how you intend to increase awareness of what you are offering, what mix of marketing strategy and tools, such as products, price, place, and promotion you will use to help you deliver the needed benefits to your customers and beat the competition.

V. Be ready to explain how you price your product or service and your rationale. A breakdown of how you arrive at your price and percentage profit margins on each unit of product or service is essential. Again, estimates of the number of clients to sell to or the units of product to sell to reach break-even point or make profit should be readily available to enable you to answer any questions.

VI. Understand where you are positioned in the market and what potential opportunities you foresee that you can exploit. You must have at least some industry facts and figures to back up your assumptions and claims.

VII. Identify who your competitors are, whether they are direct or indirect, what sets you apart and how you intend to differentiate yourself and stay ahead of the competition.

VIII. Have a plan for growth with a strategy in place for all aspects of the business's daily operations and how you plan to upscale as demand increases or the business grows. It is important to highlight the risk associated with your business. A good risk analysis (SWOT) gives investors' confidence that you have thought things through.

IX. Firmly establish and confidently articulate why you are qualified or experienced to run the business, especially if you are a sole operator. If you work with a team, you will need to prove how able they are and how their skills complement each other to run the business successfully.

X. If you have videos to show they must be professionally created and ready to play. Videos must be straight to the point and as short as possible.

XI. A business card with up-to-date contact and website details. The content of your website must be up-to-date and must complement the content of the business plan.

XII. You could potentially create a password protected investor relations page on your website where only investors are given access to review more details about your business and financial projections.

XIII. You must be able to state how much of your own money you've invested or committed to the business to date.

XIV. Any sales orders to date or potential deals yet to materialize but with the strongest possibility of being secured are important to be noted to help confirm the sales potential of your products and services.

XV. Develop 2 major levels of pitch so that you are ready when an opportunity comes your way:

A) **A 30 second to 2 minute pitch.** To capture immediate attention and ignite excitement – often known as the 'elevator pitch'. This should be enough to spark some interest. Often it is at this early stage that an investor decides whether there is the possibility of a good fit to warrant you being given a bit more time to speak. If the elevator pitch does the job you might have a few more minutes to answer a few questions from the investor, followed by a possible exchange of contacts and a phone conversation after the meeting. It is at this point that an investor will often offer the entrepreneur a formal pitching opportunity with an invitation and an agreed date for a full pitch.

B) **Up to an hour long detailed face-to-face pitch.** This often involves a full pitch, with the first 10 -15 minutes allowed for you to deliver the pitch followed by an interactive Q&A session with the investor audience who may at this stage be keen to not only know the facts and figures of your business but the person behind the business – you. This may involve a bit more probing into your overall vision, drive, depth of knowledge, business model, product, management team and returns for the investor. This is basically an analysis of your business plan. To get to this level with an investor often means you have done a good job leading them from mere excitement towards a readiness to commit funds to the business subject, of course, to due diligence, negotiation of legal terms, and signing of an agreement.

XVI. Value your business with the help of accounting professionals. It is important to get this right because over valuing is a major problem that angers investors. Factor in investor risk when valuing the business.

XVII. Decide how much of the ownership of the business you are willing to part with – 10 percent, 20 percent, 25 percent or 40 percent – and for how much cash injection from investors. A good valuation should help you to derive the right percentages. How much interest are you willing to pay on a loan? What length of loan repayment will you be comfortable with to ensure you don't stifle growth and create cash short-ages, if you are going for debt funding?

XVIII. Do research to learn about the potential investors or audience you are pitching to, their investor goals, indus-try experience, what they want from an investment and the nature of their existing investment portfolio. Most of this information can be found on their website and the websites of other businesses they have invested in in the past.

Note: To maximize your time as you book appointments to meet with potential investors ensure you speak with decision makers of the investing organization or their direct appointees and also look for investors interested in your stage and market. Investors with interest in your line of business brings a lot of experience and expertise on board in addition to a cash investment.

XIX. A well written business plan with a concise executive summary which should also include all your actuals and projected financial figures - cash flow, profit and loss (showing realistic sales projections, gross profit, total expenses and net profit or loss) and balance sheet projections for 12 months up to 5 years. The sales forecast, unit cost of production, overhead costs, and break-even point should be highlighted.

XX. *Prepare well. PRACTICE! PRACTICE! PRACTICE! You simply can never over prepare for a pitch session!!!*

The above points are not exhaustive but I've covered the most important information you will need to familiarize yourself with, to equip you to deliver a perfect pitch. It is worth noting that not all pitching sessions will necessarily require that you know all of this information. However, if you are going to be good at running a business and be in business for the long haul understanding these basic foundational elements is vital for a successful journey. The least you can do is to surround yourself with people who are good at aspects of the business where you lack skills and expertise.

In the next chapter we will address the
second Master-Class Technique —
What Investors Look For In A Pitch.

CHAPTER 24

WHAT INVESTORS LOOK FOR IN A PITCH

*"Twenty-two businesses down and one more
to go. I have only two great startups written
on my short list of where I'll put my money.
All the others won't make the cut because
they don't have the necessary street smarts,
salesmanship, bounce-back ability, arrogance,
and appetite for risk."*

Barbara Corcoran, Co-Founder of Barbara Corcoran
Venture Partners and a "Shark" investor
on ABC's Shark Tank show

Just like you, an investor is someone who has worked hard to earn the cash you are asking them to invest in your business. They are, therefore, very protective of their cash, as you would expect, and often need persuading to invest in a business, even if you are the nicest person on earth or have the loftiest of ideas.

Most, if not all, investors are very much motivated by the return they will get from the business. Some of them, such as some angel investor groups go beyond investing merely for the returns and are interested in the added satisfaction of helping a specific section of the population or community, sector of the economy, or other causes of interest as explained in Chapter 8.

Having said that, let's consider a few excerpts from some well-known seasoned investors, some of whom are guests on some of the most popular primetime TV business shows to get their take on what a perfect pitch is and what they look for in a pitch.

Naval Ravikant, a Super Angel Investor with over 75 investments and co-founder of AngelList was asked in an interview with Fatema Yasmine, a technology writer, what characteristics a company must have for him to invest. *"In terms of personal investing there are three things I look for in a company. You need a great team, a huge market, and some sort of unfair advantage. …. I use Warren Buffett's criteria for assessing the Team: Intelligence, Integrity and Energy. You want someone who is really smart, very hard working and trustworthy. A lot of people forget the integrity part, because if you don't have that, then you have a really hard working crook and they will find a way to cheat you."*

Barbara Ann Corcoran, an American business-woman, investor, speaker, consultant, syndicated columnist, author, and television personality and "Shark" investor on ABC's *Shark Tank* **shared a post on LinkedIn.com** *"Spotting a Winner on Shark Tank". Barbara said, "In my five years on Shark Tank. I've learned to choose the right entrepreneur over the right business every time, and that all entrepreneurs are an odd lot but all wired the same way. The good ones have great passion and the ability to get past their failures, and* *the entrepreneurs who don't make it lack either the resilience, ambition or street smarts needed to build a business in today's tough world. …and that's what I continue to look for on Shark Tank."*

Deborah Sonia Meaden, an English business-woman, TV personality as a *"Dragon"* **investor on BBC Two's business programme Dragons' Den, advises that,** *"The key to a good pitch is to really know your stuff, be clear on what drives the business forward and to get the message across in a concise and credible way … Use your own language, don't try to be over-clever by using "insiders" jargon… Memorise key points throughout your presentation so that, if you lose your thread, you can easily pick up again. Make sure you look good and therefore feel good on the day … Take time with your grooming in the morning, make sure you feel "a million dollars"… Be yourself and be honest."* To read more about Deborah Meaden visit deborah-meaden.com.

Daymond Garfield John, an American entrepreneur, investor, author, motivational speaker and television personality as a "Shark" investor on ABC's *Shark Tank.* **In a Q&A session by** ABC.com. **Daymond said, when asked for his advice on how to pitch and what makes a good pitch,** *"Understand what's in it for the person you are pitching to. Do not go into it about self-fulfillment that you want to be wealthy that you want your product out. That doesn't mean anything to the person you are pitching to. Why will one of the* *panelists or one of the people you are pitching to find value in the product? Will it enrich their lives? ...The thing that makes you most memorable to any of the Sharks are [sic] sales...If you don't have sales then you have to think of another way to resonate with the Sharks."*

Kelly Elaine Hoppen MBE, a British interior designer, author, proprietor of Kelly Hoppen Interiors, and a TV personality as a "Dragon" investor on *Dragons' Den* **responded when asked what makes a successful pitch and what she looks out for in the den:** *"Passion, empirical product knowledge, clarity, enthusiasm and a smile doesn't hurt! ...I'm all about investing in the person first so I'm looking for someone who I will be able to work with and of course an idea or product that I'm 100% behind. I want the entrepreneur to be passionate about their product and brand and be able to think outside the box, someone who will take chances and be brave to succeed."*

Mark Cuban, an American businessman, investor, and owner of the NBA's Dallas Mavericks, Landmark Theatres, and Magnolia Pictures, and the chairman of the HDTV cable network AXS TV as well as a "Shark" investor on US ABC's *Shark Tank***. In an interview with Alexa Valiente on Abcnews.go.com, Mark shared some pitching tips:** *"I hate the back story...because it's usually a way to hide the realities of the business...I want them to know the numbers ... I want it to be a product in a market that I think is differentiated and* *has an opportunity to grow. ...You got to get your point across, and, you know, if you can walk into this situation and get your point across, you know, explain your business to me, explain why I can invest, and really sell me on yourself, then you've accomplished something right there and that's a great indication."*

Peter Jones CBE, a British entrepreneur and businessman, TV personality as a "Dragon" investor on *Dragons' Den* **and on the American television series American Inventor offers the following pitching tips on his website** peter-jones.com. *"Dress appropriately...according to the job you are applying for...Be confident...have faith in yourself and your idea. Often I look to invest in an individual as much as in their concept. ...Be honest about your company and your forecasts. ... Do not over-estimate your capability. ...Be concise. Make sure that your business plan can be easily understood by those who you are pitching to and do not waffle. My final, and perhaps my most crucial tip of all, is make sure that you research your idea thoroughly!"*

Robert Herjavec, a Croatian-born Canadian businessman, investor, and media personality – also as a "Shark" investor on ABC's *Shark Tank.* **In one of his posts on LinkedIn.com** *"What's in a Perfect Shark Tank Pitch?"* **Robert shared his thoughts on what constitutes a perfect pitch. He said,** *"a perfect pitch is when people know their numbers, capture my fleeting attention quickly, feed* *me when I'm hungry (which is most of the time), and allow me to interact…! But most importantly, you need to be passionate, from the look in your eyes through to every cell in your body. Not only does this motivate me to invest in a product, but it motivates me in my daily life… If they've got drive, I never worry about getting a return on my investment."*

In a Q&A section on the Dragons' Den show website, in answer to the question 'What do you hope for when an entrepreneur walks into the den?' Duncan Walker Bannatyne OBE, a Scottish entrepreneur, philanthropist, author and a TV personality as a "Dragon" investor on *Dragons' Den***, said,** *"Ideally a good investment that my team and I can help grow into a successful business. I also want to be able to connect with the entrepreneur(s) and for the entrepreneur(s) to be confident and know their business specially the numbers."*

Piers Linney, a British businessman, current Co-CEO of the cloud-based IT business Outsourcery, and a TV personality as a "Dragon" investor, when asked 'what makes a successful business pitch said, *"Confidently and quickly explaining the product or service, how you will make money and making a personal impression."*

The similarities in what investors look for in a pitch are striking whether you are applying to an angel investor, angel investor group, venture capitalist, a crowdfunding platform or grant provider for funds but there are also subtle differences in the focus of the major investor categories - Equity Investors and Debt Funders – as well as what grant providers also look for in a pitch. It is part of the reason why you must take time to research your ideal investor before pitching your idea or business to them.

Let's take a look at some of the essential factors each category look for in a business plan or proposal and the pitch.

Equity Investors

Angel investors and venture capitalist organizations invest their money in return for a stake in the ownership of the business. They therefore expect to share in the rewards by way of profits and dividends. They are often keen on high growth businesses with higher returns. Among the things they take into consideration are the market size, why the business is compelling, the plan, management team, and exit strategy.

They also like to know the following in much more detail.

- Clearly stated goals of the business, where your company is right now and where it's going.

- Stage of growth of the business – seed stage, early stage startup, formative, later or expansion stage of growth in the business.

- Do you know your product or service and the inside out workings of your company, your competition, your market and its development growth plan?

- Does your product stand out in the market with unique qualities, function, or design? Are your products patented thereby creating a high barrier to entry which is not easily replicated?

- Do you have a working prototype with detailed costs of the components broken down in sections as well as the savings to be attained when mass produced in volumes?

- Do you have a business model that clearly articulates how you make money out of your products or services?

- Do you have a large or significant market for the product?

- Do you have a campaign strategy to promote the product with well-designed logos, colours and slogan to help reinforce the image of your product to make it attractive to your target market?

- Have you gained some traction in the market or generated significant buzz or interest before seeking investor support?

- Are you a person of integrity and can you be trusted?

- Are you passionate about your business and totally committed to the company and its goals?

- Are you a person they can get along with?

- Is there a clearly identifiable niche in the market that you are targeting?

- Do you have any experience in the business or industry? How do your qualifications and past experience and that of your management team complement each other in the running and managing of a successful business? Is your team committed to the business and do they have defined roles?

- What is the percentage margin on each product or service sold or to be sold? Have you made any sales yet, made a profit or do you have a plan to show when you will be able to make a profit?

- What is the expected return on investment? Professional investors often look to make between 30-50 percent annual compound growth on their investment. The numbers are very important to every investor.

- Do you know what funds are required in the short, medium and long term?

- What other sources of finance do you have? Who else are you borrowing from? Who else is investing in the business?

- What you will use the funds for, and what will this accomplish for growth?

- What percentage of ownership are you willing to give up to investors?

- What milestones or conditions are you willing to accept?

- What financial reporting is available? What information are you able to provide for scrutiny?

- Are you ready to allow investors on the board or in management to help manage the business? What roles will they play?

- Can investors add value and will you consider their input and make a reasoned decision based on your views and theirs?

- What is your exit strategy for the investor (buyback, sale, or IPO)?

Debt Funders

Unlike equity investors, banks and other debt lenders are more focused on the assurance of orderly repayment. In addition to the points raised by Equity Investors, they require the following detailed information.

- Do you have good personal and business credit? Lenders want to know who you are, how long you've been in business (if you have), and your history of meeting your financial obligations. This is largely because if you are a small business, in the eyes of the lending party, you are 'the business'. It is assumed that how you've handled your affairs in the past is a good indicator of how you'll handle your business in the future.

- The amount of loan required and how the funds will be used, what the funds will accomplish and how the money will improve your business' cashflow position and profitability, thereby ensuring repayment.

- A cashflow statement (both actuals and forecast) sufficient to enable you to repay comfortably the loan and interest within the agreed repayment period.

- A new business owner will need to provide evidence that they have a track record of profitability and success in owning or managing a similar business, even if it's in another sector.

- Requested repayment terms (number of years to repay). You will probably not have much negotiating room on interest rates but you may be able to negotiate a longer repayment term which will help cash flow.

- Proof of sufficient assets and other financial reserves as collateral and a list of all existing liabilities against the collateral, if any, to back the loan.

- Your ability to handle known risk factors and how you plan to manage those that you may encounter in the future.

- And finally, the all-important, well written, objective, accurate, believable, concise and compelling business plan to support your application.

When all is said and done, investors and lenders are keen to find out if you seem credible, trustworthy, knowledgeable about your business and industry, able to pay back the money they are considering lending you, and ultimately whether, as the person making the business decisions, you know what you are doing. Previous management experience and transferable skills from other business interests are important or, if you personally lack that convincing track record, your ability and willingness to hire better qualified and experienced people to help manage the business – at least in the interim – until you are capable. All of these factors are very important and will be seriously considered by investors and lenders.

Grant Providers

Grant providers such as governments, local authorities, private foundations and trusts often have an aim for the grant being provided such as the development of a sector of the economy, a geographic region or promoting the creation of businesses in an economically disadvantaged area with high unemployment. Most providers have different motivations for providing grants to entrepreneurs and this should be carefully researched before making an application.

Other than the viability of the project or business, grant providers will check the following.

- Whether your project or business is set up in their catchment area as most grant allocations are usually dependent in part on the location of the activity for which funding is being sought.

- Does your business or project fall under the sector or industry of the grant provider's interest? Although many grants are available across all sectors, most have specific activities of interest such as the promotion of agriculture, technology, arts and tourism-related businesses or projects.

- Clearly stated goal of the business with a specific vision of what the business seeks to do, how it seeks to achieve its goals, and the benefits the target group or clients will derive from the project. More importantly, does the business fit into the grant provider's objectives because the focus of the proposed project or business is a very important factor for consideration by almost all grant providers. A provider may be solely interested in a project or business focused on research and development, community development, regeneration, export, employment generation, or training and skills development, such as the apprenticeship promotion.

- Do you understand precisely the nature and purpose of the project or business?

- What stage of growth is the business in – seed stage, early stage startup, formative, later or expansion stage? Grants are often aimed at businesses or groups of a certain size, stage of growth, employing a minimum or maximum numbers of people, self-employed individuals or growing businesses.

- Are the finances of the organization in order or properly managed in line with existing regulations?

- Amount of funds required if there is no specific amount being offered. Grant providers often have specific amounts you can apply for and sometimes it's much less than what you need. You will be expected to explain what you will use the funds for and what this will accomplish for growth in your business

- What other sources of finance do you have? Who else are you borrowing from? Who else is investing in the business?

- Because most grant providers fund only a percentage of the total cost of a project they often like to know if you have enough resources to match the funds being requested.

- Do you have any experience in the business or industry? How do your qualifications and past experience and that of your management team complement each other in the running and managing of a successful business? Is your team committed to the business and do they have defined roles? Are they committed and dedicated to the project or business?

- Are you lacking in any skills and are you willing to undertake training as most providers offer training and skills development.

- Is there interest in your product and services?

- Are you willing and able to meet set milestones, timescales and conditions of the grant provider?

- Is your organization or business well-run with structures and systems in place?

- Do you have a business plan to drive the business or project?

For your grant application to stand a chance it must fully meet the funders' objectives; these often accompany the application guidelines. Grant providers have a number of similar interests such as a well-run organization with clear goals and sound management. They are not focused on your ability to pay back or service the debt but rather your ability to meet the funders' objectives.

As the saying goes *"just because you can bake bread does not mean you can run a bakery".* That is pretty much how most investors, lenders and grant providers think when it comes to assessing your ability to run the business or manage the project successfully. It is your sole responsibility to convince them otherwise and to demonstrate that you are the best *"horse in the race worth their bet".*

Let's turn our attention to the
third Master-Class Technique —
What Not To Do When Pitching.

CHAPTER 25

WHAT NOT TO DO WHEN PITCHING

"Regardless of the changes in technology, the market for well-crafted messages will always have an audience."

Steve Burnett, The Burnett Group

After you have invested time and resources to put together a well written, objective, accurate, believable, concise and compelling business plan; confirmed all information in the plan is up-to-date; made sure that the supporting videos and audio files are working properly and the appendices and any other supporting documents are in place; updated contact details and references; and confirmed that prototypes or samples (if you have any) are working, it's time to prepare for 'D' day.

The time to deliver a master-class pitch that will not only wow your audience but convince them to join in your quest to build a successful business empire has finally arrived.

Before we proceed, let me emphasize that the pitching techniques that we are talking about are applicable to many pitching scenarios: an impromptu elevator pitch, a pre-planned hour-long session or a business pitching contest where participants compete for cash and other prizes to fund their business. Examples of pitching contests are: the *London*

Evening Standard's (UK) **'Frontline London Campaign'** which selects 10 social entrepreneurs from youths with troubled backgrounds; the Black Enterprise **'The Best Pitch Contest'** (US) where contestants pitch their business idea before a panel of angel investors and a live audience for a chance to win valuable prizes and business resources; and **Goldman Sachs'10,000 Small Businesses program** where participants are asked to present an elevator pitch to one of the program's advisory board members, such as **Warren Buffet** "the Oracle of Omaha".

As we work our way towards delivering a master-class pitch, let's take a quick look at what **NOT TO DO** at a pitching session.

- Do not be arrogant, rude, disrespectful or cause any offence to your investor audience.

- Avoid taking things personally or getting too absorbed emotionally in your presentation or when receiving comments from your audience.

- Do not allow yourself to become angry, defensive or reactive because most investors will immediately move on if you don't appear open to comments, suggestions and feedback. You may also miss valuable insights and perspectives that could open your eyes to a new opportunity or potential pitfall.

- Do not insult the intelligence of the investor audience by using industry jargon that requires an advanced degree or expert knowledge to understand. Using too many buzzwords and clichés also makes you sound fake to many people.

- Think before you open your mouth to speak. In other words do not talk until you've thought through a question well enough to have the best possible answer for your audience.

- Do not try to be 'smart' or 'pull the wool' over the eyes of the investors.

- Never go to a pitch unprepared or with unverifiable information or supporting documents.

- Never assume you know it all and be ready to listen to any advice offered even if you do not get an investment.

- It is detrimental and naive to assume there is no competition of any kind and that your product or service is the only thing that 'has ever been'.

- Do not be scared or timid.

- Do not be over confident.

- Do not tell irrelevant back stories or meander around the point. Go straight to the point.

- Avoid generalizations and irrelevant assumptions.

- Don't skimp on industry analysis. Wherever possible use credible and well known sources for the information and facts you are presenting.

- Avoid overestimating revenues, underestimating or overlooking costs and consequently presenting over-optimistic cash flow figures. You should NEVER get your numbers wrong.

- Avoid complications or ambiguities of any kind in your delivery.

- Avoid over elaboration. Interested investors will always ask you more detailed questions after your pitch if they want more information.

- And finally, whatever you do, ensure you do not over value your business. Your valuation must factor in investor risk. It's one of the things that irritates investors the most, especially equity investors.

Avoiding the above will make a huge difference to whether the investor audience will be sold on your business prospect or not.

In the next chapter we will discuss the
fourth Master-Class Technique —
Aiming for the Perfect Pitch.

CHAPTER 26

AIMING FOR THE PERFECT PITCH

"The minute you get away from the fundamentals – whether it's proper technique, work ethic, or mental preparation – the bottom can fall out of your game."

Michael Jordan an American former professional basketball player, entrepreneur, and principal owner and chairman of the Charlotte Hornets

As discussed in Part 2, there are funds available to help entrepreneurs and startups to launch their business or to help existing businesses to grow and expand. For most entrepreneurs once the funding source that is best suited for their business has been identified the next logical step is to apply for such funds. In most cases this will require a written or live pitch to be made to the targeted investor audience to win them over for their support and cash investment.

Investors on the other hand, really care about whether your business is a smart investment because it is the potential returns that are of real interest to them.

As you prepare to deliver your winning pitch, you should also note that, for an investor, one of the biggest positives is your ability to show that you've been able to begin implementing

Investors on the other hand, really care about whether your business is a smart investment because it is the potential returns that are of real interest to them.

your idea and have potentially bagged some sales or gained some traction even if you are not ready to fully participate in the market. It could be selling some of your products or securing orders in advance; gaining some buzz or excitement about your product in the market; applying for and securing a patent; carefully researching the market; developing samples or prototypes; or investing significant time and personal resources into the business to date. To most investors, this is the bare minimum needed to demonstrate your commitment to making your business dream a success.

After analysing what a business pitch is, how to prepare for it, what investors look for in a pitch and what not to do when pitching to an investor audience, it is time to look at what to **AIM** for in your delivery: what you must do to project yourself and the business and standout positively and convincingly so that the investor audience takes notice. You can have all the facts and details to hand but

You can have all the facts and details to hand but if you are not able to "paint the kind of picture" that will leave a lasting and positive impression on the audience you will fail.

152

if you are not able to "paint the kind of picture" that will leave a lasting and positive impression on the audience you will fail.

If you have truly applied yourself up to this point and followed all that I have shared in this book, then the next step is to build on that investment in time and resources and prepare to execute an outstanding and effective master-class pitch, just like a professional.

To be effective in your delivery, you must do the following.

- Make a good impression at all times, from your outfit, personality and tone of your language, whether in a live pitch or in a recorded video pitch.

- Connect with your investor audience right from the onset.

- "Sell" you, your idea, your vision and what the investor or audience stand to gain for supporting what you are pitching to them.

- Demonstrate the professionalism that you will apply to running a successful business.

- Demonstrate how to communicate effectively. Be clear, concise, specific and compelling in your delivery. Adopt simple but strong language, phrases and words that drive home your point clearly and are memorable.

- Show that you "know your stuff" – your product, industry, market, competition and what it will take to succeed. Anything less than this is simply unacceptable to an investor. *"If you don't know what you are doing, how can we commit our resources to help you"* is pretty much how investors think. Knowing your stuff will also give you a great source of confidence during your delivery.

- Match your offer to the investor's profile. Show that you have researched your audience, know what sector and stage of business they are most interested in, as well as their geographic region of interest. Spending all your time pitching to an investor whose interest is in another sector and industry, stage of business, economic region, state, province, nation or continent is a complete waste of time and resources. Get to know what they look for in an investment opportunity and ensure you capture that in your presentation. If, for instance, regeneration of an area, cutting CO_2 emissions, other environmental issues or creation of employment opportunities for a community is a major factor in their considerations, seek to highlight any such benefits from your products and services or the way you do business as you deliver the pitch.

- Frame your pitch with a relevant and compelling story. Weave it through the pitch. Great presenters tell stories that grab the audience's attention from the beginning to the end. The story must be interesting and worth listening to. It's what makes a pitch memorable, one that remains in the mind of the audience long after you are gone. A real attention-grabbing opening and a powerful closing will help do just that.

- Be passionate, persuasive and convincing. This means making your audience know exactly how you feel about your business, the problem it solves, the value it adds to clients' lives, the joy or convenience it brings to users or customer's lives.

■ How committed you and your team are must be unquestionably evident. Your commitment to the success of the business must be driven by your love for what you do more than the money to be made. Explain why you love what you do and your belief in it. Emphasizing the personal sacrifices and resources you have personally committed to the business over time is an added advantage

■ Be pleasant and respectful. A pleasant personality carries a lot of clout and can win over investors, even if your business proposition is not very attractive to an investor. Most investors will tell you that they always assess the people behind the business first. Robert Herjavec, Founder and CEO, The Herjavec Group and a 'Shark' on ABC's *Shark Tank* show (US) once said, *"I watch the entrepreneurs very closely. I will attack the business idea, not the person, but I have a keen eye for the type of entrepreneur that I like to work with. If they've got drive, I never worry about getting a return on my investment."*

■ Be honest, authentic and credible. Of course, you cannot necessarily become authentic, honest and credible overnight because of the pitch, if you are not so already. However, if these are traits you have developed they must be reflected in all you do and say, from your values and philosophy to the way you approach business. These attributes are a must for long term business success. For the investor who potentially may only have met you on the day of the pitch, it is important to them to know who you really are and whether you can be trusted enough before they commit their cash to your business or enter into a partnership with you. Business relationships are based on trust. If you can be seen to be credible and honest most people will find it easy to commit to doing business with you. That is why it is important to be authentic - the best "you"- and not a copy of anyone else.

- Demonstrate confidence and thoughtfulness. Keep your nerve and be enthusiastic but don't become over enthusiastic or over confident. Remember always that you are having a great chat with your audience not a debate or an argument, and that it's a conversation albeit a professional business conversation to share a fantastic opportunity with them.

- Appeal to your audience on an emotional level as much as you can, and don't bombard them with facts and figures just because you need them to give you some money.

- If you have to do a live demonstration, aim at a flawless demonstration. You can only do so by practicing your pitch beforehand. As the saying goes "Practice makes perfect". And remember, you can never practice too many times.

- If you make a mistake, stop, reorganize yourself and go for it again. Do not panic, it's not the end of the world.

- It is said that audiences are likely to remember about 10 percent of what you say. It is therefore very important to leave them with a memorable sentence or phrase and a storyline that you want them to talk about or think through, even after you are gone.

Something that will fuel their curiosity and encourage them to give you more time and attention to delve more into your offer.

Establish in your mind that the investor audience is a potential partner and not an enemy set on spoiling your "pitching party". Doing all of the things we've talked about in this chapter will help you to deliver the kind of pitch capable of winning the right support and financial backing for your business.

Ultimately, the pitch must interest, inform and win over the investor audience so that they want to join with you to drive your business forward successfully, in an opportunity they cannot resist.

In the next chapter we will discuss the
fifth Master-Class Technique —
Effective Communication Style.

CHAPTER 27

EFFECTIVE COMMUNICATION STYLE

"The two words 'information' and 'communication' are often used interchangeably, but they signify quite different things. Information is giving out; communication is getting through."

Sydney J. Harris (late) an American journalist
for the Chicago Daily News
and the Chicago Sun-Times

To pitch successfully requires that you adopt the best communication style, including the right body language to enable you effectively win over the investor audience.

According to researchers, humans produce up to 700,000 different signs (Mario Andrew Pei, an Italian-American linguist and polyglot), can make and recognise approximately 250,000 facial expressions (anthropologist Ray Birdwhistell), 5,000 distinct hand gestures (M. H. Krout, researcher), and 1,000 different postures and their accompanying gestures (G. W. Hughes, researcher in Kinesics).

Also, according to Albert H Mehrabian, a Professor Emeritus of Psychology, UCLA words account for only 7% of communication, tone of voice for 38% and body language for 55% - this is known as the 7%-38%-55% Rule. A study by Wharton

University (USA) also revealed that the human eye takes in about 82 percent of what is communicated, the ears 11 percent and other senses 7 percent. The study also suggested that we can retain 10% of what we hear and 51% of what we hear and see at the same time. Generally, there are also 6 universal visual signals – anger, surprise, fear, disgust, happiness and sadness.

The question is, which combination of the above can help you to deliver an excellent and effective pitch?

Body language can be defined as various forms of nonverbal communication with or without words. Nonverbal communication can include facial expressions, gestures, body posture, eye movements or silent actions. A person's physical behaviour may reveal clues as to some unspoken intention or feelings.

In the business world body language can cause both positive and negative effects in communication. *"In the business setting, people can see what you are not saying. If your body language doesn't match your words, you are wasting your time."* **Lidia Ramse**, Business Etiquette expert.

Having said that, every individual has their own communication style and a person's delivery style can also be influenced by the type of business or who they are pitching to. A web based business or software business, will require a slightly different way of pitching than a clothing design business or a farming business. In the same way, a pitching competition to win a cash award is different from pitching to an angel investor or a venture capitalist.

The fundamental principles as explained in this book are, however, the same. Your aim must be to adapt the best possible delivery style, one that you are most comfortable with, to enable you to articulate concisely and convincingly the essential information needed to capture investor audience attention and involvement and win them over.

To deliver a successful pitch you must align your body language and your content and seek to establish a relationship of trust as quickly as possible through the way you communicate with your audience.

To deliver a successful pitch you must align your body language and your content and seek to establish a relationship of trust as quickly as possible through the way you communicate with your audience.

Your focus must be primarily on the audience and not on the content of your slides. Let's look at a few areas that you can work on to achieve maximum success in your pitch delivery.

- **Establish eye contact.** The eyes are one of the most powerful components of body language. They can express everything from interest and happiness to anger and pain. Maintaining eye contact enables you to connect with your investor audience, shows your interest, honesty and forthrightness. Failure to make eye contact gives the impression that you are hiding something or are not interested. Avoid staring at all cost as it's also often interpreted as being too aggressive.

- **Handshakes often come into play as a signal of goodwill** at the beginning of an interaction or agreement at the end. A firm handshake is important and seen as an expression of sincerity in some cultures while in others a handshake is not the most appropriate way of going about this all important opening and closing gesture. This is just one example of why you must make an effort to research your audience as cultural insensitivities can result in unwanted consequences.

- **Facial expression.** A smile adds warmth, a feeling of confidence and sends a positive message. It is appropriate most of the time, except of course in a life or death situation. Communications, such as a pitch, delivered with a smiling face will have a totally different impact to those delivered with an angry or frowning face. Mouth movements also give clues: pursing lips together can indicate that you are thinking about what you are hearing; twisting of your lips may give an indication of holding something back.

- **Tone of voice.** When we speak, other people do not just hear what we say, but how we say it. A voice that is moderate in tone, slow and clear, that projects confidence, interest and warmth has a better chance of being received than one that is unclear, strained and shaky. Listeners also pay more attention to your tone, how loud you speak, the pace and inflection. It is important to get the right balance to ensure you do not disengage with your audience. Of course it's not a speech competition but you want to be as welcoming as possible and avoid putting off your listeners before they have even considered what you have to offer.

- **Body posture and movements.** To be seen as alert and enthusiastic you must sit or stand erect. A slumped posture may indicate tiredness and also may be taken as weakness or insecurity. A lot of general body movements, such as pacing should be avoided at all cost as this is also an indication of nervousness. Only use a hand gesture when necessary in a demonstration. You want to be well composed and have as little movement as possible during your pitch to avoid distracting your audience's focus and attention.

- **Body angle,** such as keeping your head straight, makes you appear self-assured and authoritative and helps you to be taken seriously. Tilting your head to one side suggests friendliness and openness but although it may look friendly, choose the better option of keeping your head straight as it's the best way to convey professionalism and seriousness. Nodding your head every now and then is another way to affirm that you are listening. Leaning in signals your eagerness to hear more, whereas leaning away signals you've heard enough of what's being said.

- **Position of arms and legs.** The best place for your arms is by your side when standing and on the table when sitting. The preferred professional position is feet flat on the floor or legs crossed at the ankles. This makes you look confident and relaxed. Avoid positioning or resting one leg or ankle on top of your other knee or ankle if you are sitting. This can make you look arrogant. Folding your arms over your chest or crossing your legs also suggests that you have shut other people out and have no interest in them or what they are saying. This can also be interpreted as disagreement with your audience or even being in a defensive mode. You should also make every effort to keep your hands out of your pockets and avoid putting them behind your back. Fidgeting with your hair or clothes, holding your chin or rubbing your face is unprofessional and shows lack of conviction. No matter how nervous you might be, now is not the time to show it.

- **Distance or space** between you and another person is worth evaluating. It is often advisable to gauge the situation with the aim of doing whatever makes the other person feel comfortable. Standing too close is often seen as "being in someone's'" face and being pushy. On the other hand, to position yourself too far away may make you seem unwelcoming or aloof. If you find the other person keeps backing away from you as you speak to them, it might be that you are encroaching on their personal space and you may need to back off a bit.

Although you may not always be aware of what you are saying with your body, others will get the message. It is essential that the message you intend to send is exactly what you are sending. Whatever you do, practice these basic communication and body language techniques until they feel natural and always seek to use the right combination of verbal and nonverbal communication to achieve success in your business. As clearly articulated by **Jim Rohn**, an American entrepreneur, author and motivational speaker, *"Take advantage of every opportunity to practice your communication skills so that when important occasions arise, you will have the gift, the style, the sharpness, the clarity, and the emotions to affect other people."* Jim couldn't have said it any better than this.

Finally, having adequately addressed all the above, now is the time to discuss the
sixth and final Master-Class Technique —
The Master-Class Delivery.

CHAPTER 28

THE MASTER-CLASS DELIVERY

"I need to invest in founders who know how to communicate."

Barbara Corcoran, Co-Founder of
Barbara Corcoran Venture Partners
and a "Shark" investor on
ABC's Shark Tank show

As we have established in previous chapters, one of the most basic but important things a businessperson must do is to learn how to speak about their business to others, confidently and clearly, at every opportunity. The art of delivering such an effortless pitch is too important to ignore. Knowing how to do it effectively to get the desired result is the key.

Having gone through your business plan over and over again and after preparing thoroughly for your presentation, the temptation will be to talk about everything about your business in your pitch. The best way to avoid that is to know exactly what should be included in your pitch.

The Elevator Pitch

Preceding almost every pitching session is the "elevator pitch" moment. This acts as a window of opportunity that an entrepreneur or business owner must grab and "nail" if they are ever going to be given the chance to deliver a fully crafted pitch at an official investor meeting. The elevator pitch is also used to create interest in a project, idea or product, or in yourself and your expertise, at a chance meeting at your local club or pub, coffee shop, dinner party, shopping center or a business networking event with an investor, client, supplier or anyone with potential interest in your business.

The elevator pitch should leave your listeners interested, impressed and eager to hear more. It must push the right buttons, fuel the interest of the investor audience and give you a foot in the door.

The elevator pitch is therefore the first step in the process. It is an introduction to a full pitch. The aim is to cover only essential information about you and your business. It should sound very interesting, be concise, efficient, effective, and compelling. It should basically state and explain briefly:

- what your business is;
- the problem it solves;
- why it has potential for growth;
- and why you are the best person to run it successfully.

The elevator pitch should leave your listeners interested, impressed and eager to hear more. It must push the right buttons, fuel the interest of the investor audience and give you a foot in the door. Its effectiveness is dependent not only on the facts but on how creative you are in your delivery. Basic facts that can be included are:

- the name and location of your business;

- the problem your business solves;

- what your product or service is;

- benefits to customers or clients - the solution you provide, cost savings, or the convenience your product offers users;

- market size and target market – businesses or individual clients;

- what sets you apart: product, service delivery or both;

- how many sales to date, number of clients on your books, or users to date;

- the quality of your team;

- where you are going and what you need to get there.

Your ability to deliver this passionately and in an exciting way in under 2 minutes is critical. Of course, if it's a pitching competition or a contest you should always look out for the rules or guidelines provided as you work your way through the above outline.

Full Pitch

After a successful elevator pitch an entrepreneur is often given the chance to make a full pitch, usually involving a face-to-face pre-booked session.

Making a success of this opportunity is dependent on what you include in the pitch and a delivery style that wins over the investor audience. The outline below should enable you to capture all the essential aspects of the business for a well-crafted pitch. The aim should be to adequately capture everything in 10-15 minutes although the session itself could stretch up to an hour with Q&A for further clarification and explanation

For the avid fans of the ABC's *Shark Tank* show (US) or the BBC *Dragons' Den* show (UK), there is often a misconception that every pitch is as portrayed on TV. It is worth noting that this is not the case. What is shown on TV is a heavily edited version of the full pitch which can take up to two hours in some cases to shoot but is condensed into a few minutes for the sake of TV.

Always remember to have copies of your business plan ready on request, preferably one for every investor, if there is more than one in the audience.

To be effective and to do it right you must bear in mind the points we have discussed in *'What Not To Do When Pitching'* (Chapter 25) and *'Aiming for the Perfect Pitch'* (Chapter 26). Be creative and try to make your audience follow your story and participate in the unfolding of the idea, concept or business you are pitching to them.

Always remember to have copies of your business plan ready on request, preferably one for every investor, if there is more than one in the audience.

Here is what must be included in a fully crafted pitch:

Introduction

Introduce yourself – your name, the name of your business and your business location. In a single sentence, clearly state what your organization's vision or goal is.

Specific Problem (s) You Seek To Solve

This is where you take the opportunity to clearly state the problem, pain, or challenges your specific target client or customer faces and how you are positioned to solve the problem. It is a good place to tell a real life story that captures the problem, pain or challenge in a way that your audience can relate to. Aim to clearly outline the context of the problem, the urgency of the problem and who particularly faces this problem that needs solving.

Product and/or Service

Confidently articulate what your idea, product or service is, how it works, how it solves the problem, relieves the pain, offers convenience, brings joy, cuts cost, adds value to the client's life. It must have a specific purpose and target audience. This is an opportunity to show that you know what you are doing.

Intellectual Property

Mention any intellectual property such as a trademark or patent you have applied for or license obtained for your product or service and have appropriate certification or documentation on hand for inspection where necessary.

Differentiation

Give your audience 2 to 3 specific reasons why your product, service or approach is unique (unique selling proposition or USP) such as better cost savings, design, or function. Show how different it is compared to what is already out there and how you will make customers prefer your product over the competition. Mention a few names of what is already out there by way of direct and/or indirect competitors or offers and emphasize what sets you apart from them.

Amount of Investment

State the amount of investment that you are looking for and what specific aspect of the business these funds will be applied to, the expected percentage growth rate, how much cash investment you will need to achieve these growth levels within what time frame, and when the investor can begin to expect a return.

Percentage of Equity

Understand the percentage of equity you are willing to give away for the amount you are seeking from the investor. The valuation of your business is directly linked to percentage of equity you are offering. Where possible state the expected return on investment within a possible time frame.

Market Gap & Strategy

Talk about the potential market gap out there to exploit, backed up by industry figures from credible sources. Be honest about how you arrived at the market size estimates as well as what you aim to capture. Identify how and where to find the target customer and the campaign strategy to promote the product. Highlight your marketing strategy to show how you will capture your targeted percentage share of the market.

Sales Record

State any sales figures to date, your revenue projections for the next year to five years, how many customers or clients you may have on your books and the potential rate of growth for the next couple of years. Be mindful not to promise anything extravagant and be realistic about future sales based on researched facts and data. Have a plan to show how you'll get to those targets and how the unique qualities of your product or strategy will enable you to scale up.

Financials

State the **sales**, **gross profit/loss**, **net profit/loss** figures and **cashflow** balances for the last year or two as well as projected figures for the next 12 months and yearly projections up to the next five years. Your projections must be realistic. It is important to get your figures right. If you need to memorize them, please do.

Management

This is where you sell yourself, and the skills and experience that qualifies you to run the business successfully. It is an opportunity to establish your credentials and your understanding of the industry and customer needs. If you have a management team, it is also the time to emphasize their core competencies and clearly state why they complement each other in the successful running of the business.

Conclusion

In your conclusion, thank the investor audience for the opportunity to pitch to them. Finish strongly with a memorable ending summing up why they should invest in your business and what their rich experience, advice and cash injection will add to the business. State the amount needed for what percentage of ownership you are prepared to give away (if its equity investment you are seeking). Leave them with an invitational statement such as "to take this exciting opportunity forward, I would like to discuss further how we can work together to make this a…(business name) success" and invite questions.

Q&A

Be ready to confidently and boldly answer every question your audience asks you. It is important to see the Q&A session as an opportunity to fill in any gaps in your pitch and to bring better understanding and clarity of your business idea to your audience.

Crafting The Pitch

To make the above outline work effectively for you, you must create a write-up of each section of your business under the headings provided. Work out a summary for each section. Refine each summary to capture the core of the section in two to three lines before you put all of the sections together. Once put together, develop them into the two levels of pitching discussed in Chapter 23 – Elevator (under 2 minutes) and the Full level pitch (an hour or more).

The next step is to create a clear and articulate write-up from the refined summary and fine tune it for each desired level.

Time yourself against the suggested timelines and practice your delivery.

As mentioned in the previous chapter, in any communication or dialogue how you deliver it is just as important as what you say. Practicing your refined pitch in front of your colleagues or any person who can give you candid feedback, or even in front of a mirror, is a good way to go. This should enable you to talk at the right speed, to sound natural, to adopt the right body language and remember all the essential elements. Like anything else, practice is what will make you perfect, so practice until it becomes natural to you. Continue to work to improve your delivery and tailor it for different audiences.

You must also have on hand your business cards, brochures, flyers and any such souvenir items to leave with your investor audience for them to take away. These will help them to remember you and your pitch, even after you leave.

The above should enable you deliver a confident and convincing master-class pitch that effectively captures the imagination and interest of the investor audience and entices them to support and invest in your business.

CHAPTER 29

BONUS – THE SUCCESSFUL SALES PITCH

"It is not your customer job to remember you, it is your obligation and responsibility to make sure they don't have the chance to forget you."

Patricia Fripp - Professional Keynote Speaker, Executive Speech Coach, Public Speaking Expert and Sales Presentation Trainer

The aim of this book has been to prepare you to pitch your business convincingly to potential investors and partners to win their cash support and investment backing. However, we also know that an entrepreneur's ability to survive in business and make a success of it is dependent on their ability to effectively pitch to potential clients and customers to win their business. The ability to sell is crucial to the success of any business but also surprisingly easy to get wrong.

Most entrepreneurs do not see themselves as salespersons, however, Zig Ziglar, an American author, salesman, and motivational speaker, once said, *"I have always said that everyone is in sales. Maybe you don't hold the title of salesperson, but if the business you are in requires you to deal with people, you, my friend, are in sales."*

In this bonus chapter I would like to offer a few tips and guidelines to enable you deliver an effective sales pitch.

From the **Cambridge Advanced Learner's Dictionary**, a sales pitch is defined as *"a way of talking that is intended to persuade you to buy something"*.

Ultimately an effective sales pitch must present the product or service's features, accessibility, and benefits to the prospect.

It is used to either introduce a product or service to an audience who knows nothing about it, or as a descriptive expansion of a product or service that an audience has already expressed interest in. It can be delivered either formally or informally, and can be delivered in any number of ways.

Ultimately an effective sales pitch must present the product or service's features, accessibility, and benefits to the prospect.

Just like delivering a business pitch, when it comes to a sales pitch, the question is where you start, how you approach a prospect and what you say to enable you win over the prospect and close the deal.

1) The first tip is **Know Your Product or Service** — the features and, more importantly, benefits to the customer - inside out. You must genuinely believe in your products and services and the fact that they will benefit the prospect. This will give you great confidence and also show that you really know what you are talking about. Be ready to answer any questions and prepare to address or effectively handle any

objections a prospect may raise. Some of the most common sales objections fall in four categories - budget constraints, authority, need, and timing. For instance if the client tells you they have not budgeted for it, you could delve a bit more to understand whether it's just that the price is too high, they do not fully appreciate the value of what you are offering, or take the opportunity to explain how much cash savings your product can save them. Or if they have a competing product similar to yours, hone in on what sets your product apart. Your responses must aim at reassuring them and offering them better value and benefits. Any attempts to dither and brush away a client or prospects concern will only result in loss of business.

2) Have a **Set Objective** for the sales meeting, appointment or call. Whether it's cold calling or showing up at a pre-arranged meeting, it is important to have objectives for the meeting, such as who you would like to speak to and why, the time you would like to spend on the call, what you have on offer and what your desired outcome should be. The desired outcome can be anything from arranging for another meeting to fully pitch your offer, closing the deal over the phone, placing of orders, signing up for the service, or getting contact details such as an email to send detailed information.

3) **Go After The Decision Maker.** It is very important to target and seek out the one who makes the decision to buy or not to buy. It is not prudent to spend all your time and resources booking appointments and chasing after the individual member of the household,

assistant or receptionist of an organization who has no influence on the final buying decision. **Albert S. Ruddy**, a Canadian-born film and television producer once said, *"You should get as close to the power when you're pitching something. I got my two biggest breaks with the man who owned CBS and the guy that owned Paramount, because I was dealing with the guy who would say yes or no."*

4) **Research Your Prospects.** From the outset the sales pitch should be about who you are pitching to. *"When you sell a product or service, you're making a promise to your audience. If you don't understand your audience, you'll never be able to keep that promise and you'll ultimately let them down."* — **Daymond John**, Co-founder of Fubu and "Shark" investor on the *Shark Tank* show (US). Taking the time to research your prospect should help you avoid getting lost in what your company is about, etc. Seek to know your prospect with the aim of building a relationship. Find out what they like; when they are available if an appointment is needed to meet with them, other than at a networking event or a chance meeting; how they like to engage and what potentially puts them off. Especially if it's a major prospect, not researching them can be a potential embarrassment and shut out the opportunity. As most decision makers are busy and have many other responsibilities in any given day, you wouldn't want to go in unannounced and expect them to make time for you unprepared.

5) **Get Your Prospect in the Right Setting** where they are most comfortable and relaxed to engage with you. It could be their office, favourite restaurant,

meeting venue or a coffee shop. Let them chose the right place and time if it's not a chance meeting but a pre-arranged meeting, and they're more likely to engage and potentially say yes to a deal.

6) As simple as this may sound, How You **Greet Your Prospect** makes a significant difference. It is always advisable to greet them by their name and title. It makes it much easier and less awkward than greeting them as Ma'am or Sir which may initially sound respectful but is regarded as submissive.

7) Also, as with any communication it is good to **Start the Conversation with a Relaxed Casual Pleasantry**, such as, it's a great day, I like your office or the view outside your window. Or start with something you share or have in common as a way to identify with the prospect. Whatever you say, it should be sincere and not overdone or inappropriate. Since you most certainly may not know how your prospect may take it, you must use your best judgment, be on target and be professional at all times.

8) **Go Straight to the Purpose of the Meeting** after the initial pleasantries without beating about the bush to avoid wasting your allotted time with the prospect.

9) **Be Simple and Clear** in your choice of language. Using industry or professional jargon and clichés won't do you any favors.

10) **Keep It Short and Specific** because this is more persuasive than generalizing information and facts especially when it comes to the exact help you are

willing to offer as well as the value or benefits to the prospects.

11) For most prospects the key is **Whether Your Product or Service Will Make or Save Them** Money and make their life better. Often any other benefits - such as the products "green" credentials - are essentially a bonus and secondary to the cash benefits. It is important to get your figures right and to highlight them.

12) Always remember that it is a **Two Way Conversation and Not a Lecture**. It must be approached as a dialogue with the aim of listening more and talking less. The 80/20 rule should be applied here, i.e. listening 80 percent of the time and talking 20 percent of the time during the meeting or pitch session. Even in a situation where the prospect asks you to make an initial presentation, take just the first 2 – 5 minutes to talk about the product and the potential benefits to the client in line with their needs. Aim to convince your prospect and give them enough reason

The conversation must ultimately enable you to uncover the prospect's needs, understand these needs, and show them how what you are selling can help them meet that need, fix the problem or help them accomplish what they are trying to accomplish.

to want to engage further with you. Otherwise, you should look at engaging with the prospect right from the onset, asking questions about their needs, past experiences and challenges with similar products and their interest. As emphasized by **Wendy Weiss**, Author and Sales coach, *"A good pitch is one where you ask questions, listen to the prospect, and offer them a solution to a problem."*

13) If you're smart, the next step is to **Ask For Orders** or to **Come Up With A Recommendation** for the best way forward. Make recommendations, encouraging prospects to promise to at least consider your recommendations or ask for opportunities to meet again or talk to them again if a deal is not closed at the meeting.

The goal is to get the prospect's attention and an agreement to have an engaged conversation about how you can help them with something specific in their life or business. The conversation must ultimately enable you to uncover the prospect's needs, understand these needs, and show them how what you are selling can help them meet that need, fix the problem or help them accomplish what they are trying to accomplish.

If you have to pitch before any opportunity for interaction, here are some of the things you should consider including:

- brief introduction of yourself and your business;

- what your product or service is, highlighting distinguishing features and function;

- what buyer's specific problem (having researched the client prior to the session) it solves;

- how much savings can be derived from using the products, income to be generated or relief to the customer;

- how effective it is in managing an aspect of a client's life, process or business;

- any after sales service offers.

Applying the 80/20 rule (listening more, talking less) should enable you to understand the exact needs of the prospect and to specifically respond with what you can do to help and the benefits and the value of your product, taking every opportunity to emphasize the costs savings, time savings, or percentage profits to be gained. Examples of how you helped others could also boost their confidence in what you are offering. Each pitch must therefore speak to the unique challenges of the person or business you're pitching to.

Finally, to be successful at any given sales pitch you must go in with the mind-set that you are going to have a conversation and build a relationship with the prospect and not just close a deal. *"You don't close a sale, you open a relationship if you want to build a long-term successful enterprise"* said **Patricia Fripp**, Professional keynote speaker, executive speech coach, public speaking expert and sales presentation trainer.

CHAPTER 30

CONCLUSION

Launching, starting or growing a successful business is every entrepreneur's goal. However, as with any worthwhile endeavor, you will have to work on all the essential areas to enable you build a successful business.

Pitching is one such essential skill which, when mastered, should position you - the entrepreneur - to effectively make the most of any opportunities that come your way on the journey to greater business success.

It is evident that the level of preparation and amount of practice necessary to make a success of persuading the audience is the key to winning their support.

As **Benjamin Franklin**, Founding Father of the USA, once said, *"An investment in knowledge pays the best interest."* The added advantage is that the time and resources you invest in preparing your pitch will help you to fully analyze and appreciate your business, your market, business model and strategy. If preparation is the key then the effectiveness of your delivery is the force that pushes the door open and invites investors to join you in driving your business dream forward.

Although an essential skill, most entrepreneurs are not confident of their ability to manage a pitch successfully. Even so, every entrepreneur, whether naturally gifted or not, will need to develop and master the skill because one way or the other it is the one skill that will be called on throughout the life of a business.

As pitching is also an integral part of sourcing funds, it is worth re-stating that investors expect the entrepreneur or business owner to be the one to deliver the pitch and not a representative, except of course under special circumstances. The underlying assumption is that, as the originator of the idea, concept or business, no one can be more passionate or have a fuller understanding of what the business is about than you. Making someone else deliver for you stands the risk of undermining your own ability to run the business successfully. As an entrepreneur, you wouldn't want to shoot yourself in the foot like that, would you? I don't think so. That is why pitching is such a vital skill to master to enable you, as an entrepreneur, to build a successful business.

Every entrepreneur, whether naturally gifted or not, will need to develop and master the skill because one way or the other it is the one skill that will be called on throughout the life of a business.

Pitching is also a great way to build and develop business relationships, like any networking opportunity. It gives you the chance to build your confidence as you craft your pitch and talk about your business and the transformation it brings to the lives of people. It is, therefore, good to appreciate each person you meet and to value each opportunity to talk about your business because it is simply impossible to know where the conversation will lead. These relationships can potentially yield more than just the cash investments you so desperately need. Even if an investor does not invest, they may offer to link you up to a retailer or top sales contact or to share some thoughts and ideas that could transform your business and better position you to drive the business forward successfully.

Even if an investor does not invest, they may offer to link you up to a retailer or top sales contact or to share some thoughts and ideas that could transform your business and better position you to drive the business forward successfully.

In this book, we have dealt with this all important subject – pitching - largely to investors but also in respect to pitching to potential clients and customers. I have every confidence that, as an entrepreneur, you are now well equipped to master this all important skill and will be successfully pitching your business like a pro at every opportunity.

It's now time to step out and take advantage of all the platforms you have to win investor backing and clients' business.

Wishing you GREAT SUCCESS in YOUR BUSINESS.

THANK YOU!

APPENDIX A

Some of the active angel Investor groups, networks and associations around the world to help you find angel Investors to fund your business.

Name	Country	Investment Focus	Website
Angel One Investor Network	Canada	All Entrepreneurs	angelonenetwork.ca
Golden Triangle Angel Network	Canada	All Entrepreneurs	goldentriangleangelnet.ca
Keiretsu Forum	Canada	All Entrepreneurs	keiretsutoronto.ca
VA Angels	Canada	All Entrepreneurs	vaangels.com
European Founders Fund	EU	Early Stage and Later Stage	europeanfounders.com
FiBAN Network	Finland	Early Stage Funding	fiban.org
France Angels Network	France	All Businesses	franceangels.org
Paris Business Angels	France	High Growth Companies Investing	parisbusinessangels.com
Business Angels Network	Germany	Early-Stage Funding	business-angels.de
Indian Angel Network Services Pvt Ltd	India & International	Startup and Early Stage Ventures	indianangelnetwork.com
Business Angels Network	Italy	All Businesses	iban.it
Luxembourg Business Angel Network	Luxembourg	Early Stage Investments	lban.lu
Business Angels Network	Netherlands	All Businesses	bannederland.nl

Name	Country	Investment Focus	Website
Norwegian Business Angel Network	Norway	All Businesses	norban.no
FNABA - National Federation of Business Angels	Portugal	All Businesses	fnaba.org
RUSSBA – The National Union of Business Angels of Russian Federation	Russia	Early Stages, Seed Stage and Startup Stage	russba.ru
AEBAN - Spanish Association of Business Angels Networks	Spain	All Businesses	aeban.es
Angels Den	UK	All Entrepreneurs	angelsden.com
Cambridge Capital Group – UK & International	UK & International	Specialist in Technology Startups	cambridgecapitalgroup.co.uk
Clearly Social Angels	UK	Specialist in Social Enterprises	clearlysocialangels.com
Go Beyond Ltd	UK	Early Stage Investor	go-beyond.biz
JamJar Investments	UK	All Entrepreneurs	jamjarinvestments.com
Venture Giant	UK	All Entrepreneurs	venturegiant.com
xénos Business Angel Network	Wales, UK	Growth Fund Investing	xenos.co.uk
Alliance of Angels	USA	All Entrepreneurs	allianceofangels.com
Golden Seeds	USA	Focused on Women-led Startups	goldenseeds.com
Investors' Circle	USA	Non-profits & Entrepreneurs	Investorscircle.net
SV Angel	USA	Early Stage	svangel.com

APPENDIX B

Some of the active venture capitalist groups, networks and associations around the world to help you find venture capitalists to fund your business.

Name & Main Office	Country	Funding Info.	Website
BDC Capital. Subsidiary of Business Development Bank Montreal, Quebec	Canada	Fund Size: $1B Stage: Early Stage, Expansion, Later Stage	bdc.ca/EN/bdc-capital/venture-capital
Emerald Technology Ventures Toronto, Ontario	Canada	Fund Size: $440M Stage: Early Stage, Expansion	emerald-ventures.com
GrowthWorks Ltd. Vancouver British Columbia	Canada	Fund Size: $800M Invest. Range: $0.1M - $5M Stage: Expansion	growthworks.ca
VantagePoint Venture Partners Montreal, Quebec	Canada	Fund Size: $4b Stage: Startup/ Seed, Early Stage, Expansion, Later Stage	vpcp.com
Draper Fisher Jurvetson Bangalore, Karnataka	India	Fund Size: $7B Invest. Range: <$25M Stage: Startup/ Seed, Early Stage, Growth Stage	dfj.com
TA Associates - Worli Mumbai, Maharashtra	India	Fund Size: $18B Invest. Range: $50M - $500M Stage: Expansion	ta.com
SEAVI Advent Singapore	Singapore	Fund Size: $37B Invest. Range: $10M - 25M Stage: Expansion, Later Stage	seavi.com.sg

Name & Main Office	Country	Funding Info.	Website
Apax Partners Main office – Barcelona	Spain	Fund Size: $44.2B Invest. Range: <$60M Stage: Startup/ Seed, Early Stage, Expansion, Later Stage	apax.com
3i London	UK	Fund Size: £12.9B Stage: Growth, Expansion	3i.com
Amadeus Capital Partners Ltd. London	UK	Fund Size: £8M Invest. Range: <$15M Stage: Startup/ Seed, Early Stage, Expansion, Later Stage	amadeuscapital.com
Balderton Capital London	UK	Fund Size: $2.3B Invest. Stage: $2M - $80M Stage: Early Stage	balderton.com
Accel Partners Palo Alto, California	USA	Fund Size: $8.8B Stage: Startup/ Seed, Early Stage, Growth	accel.com
Adams Street Partners Chicago, Illinois	USA	Fund Size: $22B Invest. Range: $5M - $20M Stage: Early Stage	adamsstreetpartners. com
Andreesen Horowitz Menlo Park, California	USA	Fund Size: $2.7B Invest. Range: <$50M Stage: Early Stage	a16z.com
Bain Capital Ventures Boston, Massachusetts	USA	Fund Size: $70B Invest. Range: <$60M Stage: Startup/ Seed, Early Stage, Expansion, Later Stage	baincapitalventures. com

Name & Main Office	Country	Funding Info.	Website
The Carlyle Group Washington, District of Columbia	USA	Fund Size: $199B Stage: Expansion, Early Stage	carlyle.com
D.E. Shaw Group New York, New York	USA	Fund Size: $32B Invest. Range: <$20M Stage: Early Stage	deshaw.com
Element Partners Radnor, Pennsylvania	USA	Fund Size: $12.5B Invest. Range: $10M - $50M Stage: Early Stage	elementpartners.com
First Round Capital Philadelphia, Pennsylvania	USA	Fund Size: $2.5B Stage: Seed-Stage	firstround.com
General Catalyst Partners Cambridge, Massachusetts	USA	Stage: Early Stage, Growth Stage	generalcatalyst.com
Kleiner Perkins Caufield & Byers (KPCB) Menlo Park, California	USA	Stage: Incubation, Early Stage	kpcb.com
Lightspeed Venture Partners	USA	Fund Size: $2B Stage: Early Expansion	lsvp.com
New Enterprise Associates Menlo Park, California	USA	Fund Size: $14B Invest. Range: <$100M Stage: Startup/ Seed, Early Stage, Expansion, Later Stage	nea.com
Sequoia Capital Main office Menlo Park, California	USA	Fund Size: $2.4B Invest. Range: $0.1M - $10M Stage: Incubation, Seed Stage, Startup, Early Stage, Growth Stage	sequoiacap.com

Name & Main Office	Country	Funding Info.	Website
Signal Lake Management LLC Westport, Connecticut	USA	Fund Size: $60B Invest. Range: $0.1M - $100M Stage: Early Stage	signallake.com
Summit Partners Boston, Massachusetts	USA	Fund Size: $16B Invest. Range: $5M - $500M Stage: Expansion	summitpartners.com
SVB Capital Palo Alto, California	USA	Fund Size: $23B Stage: Startup/Seed Early Stage	svb.com/svbcapital
Warburg Pincusis San Francisco, California	USA	Fund Size: $37B Invest. Range: <$2M Stage: Startup/ Seed, Early Stage, Expansion, Later Stage	warburgpincus.com
Y Combinator Mountain View, California	USA	Invest. Range: <$0.02M Stage: Startup/ Seed Stage	ycombinator.com
Google Ventures	USA & EU	Fund Size: $1.5B Stage: Seed Venture, Growth Stage	gv.com

APPENDIX C

List of some of the active global crowdfunding sites to help you set up campaigns to raise funds for your business and other causes.

Name	Country	Type of Platform	Market
Assob.com.au	Australia	Equity	General
FundedByMe.com	European Union	Equity	Startups, SME, Growth
Invesdor.com	Northern Europe	Equity	Growth Stage
Venturebonsai.com	Finland	Equity	Startups
Afexios.com	France	Equity	General
MIPISE.com	France	Equity, Rewards, Revenue Share	Startups
WiSEED.com/fr	France	Equity	Startups
Companisto.de	Germany	Equity	Startups
Innovestment.de	Germany	Equity Auction	Startup
Seedmatch.de	Germany	Equity	Startups and Small Business
Starteed.com	Italy	Revenue - Share	General
Gambitious.com	Netherlands	Equity	Gaming
Symbid.com	Netherlands	Equity	Startups
Thrillcapital.com	New Zealand	Equity	Niche/Sports
Sociosinversores.es	Spain	Equity	Startups
C-crowd.com	Switzerland	Equity	General
Eureeca.com	United Arab Emirates	Equity	General
Abundancegeneration.com	United Kingdom	Revenue-Share	Niche/Solar
BankToTheFuture.com	United Kingdom	Equity, Debt	Small Business
Crowdcube.com	United Kingdom	Equity	Startups
FundingCircle.com	United Kingdom	Debt	Small Business
Growthfunders.com	United Kingdom	Equity, Rewards	Businesses

Name	Country	Type of Platform	Market
Seedrs.com	United Kingdom	Equity	Startups
TrillionFund.com	United Kingdom	Equity, Rewards & Debt	General
Angel.co	United States	Equity, Debt	Startup
Crowdfunder.com	United States	Equity	Startups
Fundable.com	United States	Equity, Rewards & Debt	Small Business
Gofundme.com	United States	Rewards	General
Indiegogo.com	United States	Rewards	General
JoinMosaic.com	United States	Debt	Solar Projects
Kickstarter.com	United States	Rewards	Projects Only
MicroVentures.com	United States	Equity	Startups
Rockethub.com	United States	Rewards	General
Seedups.com	United States, United Kingdom, Ireland, Canada	Equity	Startups
StartSomeGood.com	United States	Rewards	Startups
Startupaddict.com	United States	Equity	Startups
Wefunder.me	United States	Equity	Startups

ABOUT THE AUTHOR

Victor Kwegyir is an international business consultant, business coach, entrepreneur, business motivational speaker, author, the founder and CEO of Vike Invest Ltd, a growing International Business Consultancy firm in London, UK. He has over eighteen years' experience in business, and holds a Master's degree (MSc in International Financial Systems) with other qualifications.

He speaks internationally at seminars, challenging and equipping people with the knowledge and practical tools in starting and growing successful businesses. Victor is a regular guest speaker and contributor to entrepreneurial development and business growth & profitability radio shows (over 60 guest appearances). He also has his own blog as well as contributes to other blogs and business finance and management websites around the world.

In addition to this book, Victor has also authored such books as "The Business You Can Start – Spotting the greatest opportunities in the economic downturn" and co-authored "You've Been Fired! Now What? - Seize the opportunity, creatively turn it into a successful reality"- available on Amazon, Kindle, ITunes, iBookstore, Nooks, Sony Reader - eBook edition, Barnes and Nobles, Vikebusinessservices.com and book stores near you (just ask the store attendant).

Victor's other upcoming books include, "Starting the business right" and "Wealth creation as God intended."

To request Victor for one-on-one business coaching and consultation services, speaking engagements, and interviews please send an email to victor@vikebusinessservices.com.

Victor's books are available at special discounts when purchased in bulk for promotions as well as for educational or fund raising activities.